Comments o

"God is still in the business of calling people to go to the Ninevehs of the world. He is still getting a variety of answers such as, 'Yes, I'll go,' but they don't show. 'Later...'...but later doesn't come. 'I'll pray about it,' and no answer. Jerald January helps us to recognize God's calling and explains how God wants to work, through people like us, to accomplish His purpose."

-- Will Perkins
Colorado for Family Values

"As a young boy in the 1960s, the vivid images of fires, marches, and black ministers crying out for equality left an indelible mark on my mind and heart. Now over 30 years later (this time as a Christian) I hear the cry coming from the heart of God. I pray that the Church will unite and show the redemptive love of God as He speaks to us *A Second Time!*"

-- Larry Yonker
Director of Development,
Compassion International

A Second Time

A Second Time

The life of Jonah and the American
church today

Jerald January

Cool Springs Publishing House
Colorado Springs, Colorado

Dedication

This book is dedicated to all the members of the Body of Christ who have lived according to the wish of our Savior to "love one another," regardless of tradition, pressure or condemnation of others.

Table of Contents

Acknowledgments

I would like to thank the Lord Jesus Christ for everything I am and will be.

To my wife Jerra, my best friend and the love of my life.
My fabulous children Chane', Craig, Jerald Jr., Charlene, and James. I look forward to seeing how God will lead your lives.

Thanks to only a few of the individuals that have blessed my life during the last year or so:
Nadine Paul, Vince & Debborha Guillory, Doris Holloway, Tommy & Darlene Moore, James & Joyce Skeet, Clarence & Brenda Shuler, Scott & Beverly Salley, Fred & Kim Hammond and all the folks at Face to Face, Fred & Regina Stokes, Sam Hooks, Will & Bess Perkins, Larry & Cassandra Norton, Ron & Eleanor Ballard, Herb & Wanda Brisbane, Alemu & Genet Beeftu, Tom & Zarette Beard, Keith & Karen Colvin, The Dandridge's, Maude Davis, Kathy Dudley, Eddie & Mary Edwards, Greg Reed,

Wally Erickson, Greg & Kelly Feste, Billy & Sarah Gaines, David & Robin Guy, A.C. Green, Calvin & Deborah Johnson, Rick Nelson, Michael & Yvonne Jones, Tim Leigh, Richard Goode, Bishop George McKinney, John & Mary Murphy, Malcom Newton, Mark & Ella Pollard, Matt Parker, Paul & Barb Robles, Willie (Dad) Vaughn, Jack & Carolyn Vaughn, Dolphus Weary, Larry & Kim Yonker, Annie Wamberg and Richard Washington.

A special thanks to our prayer partners who have given their time to pray for my family and me: Hank Davis, Delores Dillard, Denise Fairfax, Ophelia Trammell, Bob Lunden, Fred and Joyce Luthy.

And last but not least Steve Wamberg, my partner in good and one of the best editors in the world.

Editor's Note

I believe God has given Jerald January a unique message for the American church, and a distinctive approach through which to share that message.

A Second Time is a compilation of Jerald January's messages based on the book of Jonah. It has been my privilege to edit these timely sermons into a print format, and my intent to keep Jerald's enthusiasm and passion intact while offering readers chapters that bring the content to light in book form. Still, some readers (like me) might enjoy reading this work more as sermons than chapters. To recapture the messages as they are often delivered by Jerald, read the Introduction through Chapter Three, Chapter Four through Chapter Six, Chapter Seven through Chapter Nine, and Chapter Ten.

Then, of course, join us in the effort to apply God's Word in obedience to His will.

-- Steve Wamberg

Foreword

A Second Time gives you an exhilarating feeling of hope in the area of racial unity and harmony. This book identifies destructive patterns in the church of the United States that have hindered the church's efforts to be one yesterday, today, and maybe in generations to come.

By comparing the example of Jonah with that of the modern American church, Jerald January has challenged me to step up to the plate and take action, instead of standing on the sidelines and watching the demise of another community, state, or even country.

This book has forced me to ask God, "What is it you want me to do?"

He is answering, and I am committed to be a part of a fresh move of His Spirit as I seek to help achieve the ends put forth in *A Second Time* to heal His people, and this land.

A.C. Green
National Basketball Association Player & Author

Introduction

"If I'd only done it in the first place, I wouldn't be in this mess."

Who hasn't uttered that famous phrase? And you know what "it" is, too: that thing that is right to do now, but "just not convenient" to do until the future.

It's part of the human experience to find yourself doing something you should have done earlier. If you're like me, chances are you've found yourself more than once with that embarrassed look on your face. You know that look. It's all over you when you're walking down the road with that gas can in your hand, trying to appear as though you always get your exercise this way. Yeah...and you always do this workout to gas up the car. Right...and you always dress like this to go for a three-mile hike. As folks go speeding by, you smile and wave like you're saying goodnight to dinner guests.

Or maybe for you it's that sick feeling you get when you realize that the utility bill you put off paying for a few weeks is overdue. Okay, not just "overdue": the lights have been cut off and it's the weekend. Standing there, you confess to the lamp that once gave you light, "It would have only taken three minutes to mail the stupid thing in."

Procrastination is delaying your action on something you have every intention of doing. Take heart, you're not the only procrastinator in your church. You're probably not the only procrastinator in your family. (Maybe you even put off reading this book for a while. Shame on you.)

There's something curious about procrastination. Procrastination may cause some embarrassment or discomfort for those around the procrastinator -- but more

1

often than not, it harms the procrastinator more than anyone else.

God in his infinite wisdom has chosen to give us the ability to choose. We begin choosing from the time we are infants. From the type of cereal we preferred to which rattle made us smile were results of our choices. Choices continue to drive us as adults. We choose some things to amuse us; we choose other things that make us feel comfort. We even choose those things that bring us pain. All that said, God is so serious about us learning to make responsible choices that He has ultimately given us the choice of life or death.

Choices are a vital part of God's plan for us. Thanks to the freedoms and liberties that have been bestowed upon us in the United States, we have choices that many in other parts of the world can only dream of. But there are still restraints to be considered, especially due to the freedoms we enjoy.

God has demonstrated some patterns of choice that we should emulate. For instance, he has said we should be holy because he is holy. God has not changed his mind about what is best for us, even though living a holy lifestyle may not be the most popular pattern of choice today. When we choose not to mirror his conduct, nor to live according to his desire for us, we find ourselves floundering.

But understand this: it's *our* choice to disobey, so don't blame God for those results. Our chosen conduct has some temporal pleasure, but our desired results don't last. So we choose modifications to our conduct in an attempt to liven things up. Unfortunately, when God isn't included in our planning, the results are more of the same.

Every passing day reminds us of God's desire for our lives. Given that fact, it is amazing how many of us choose to trifle with our own destiny by ignoring *God's* desires. *We* desire to be happy, but we are driven by pride to stay on our own path -- a path that only leads to additional frustration and heartache. While God's voice echoes in our heart we continue to run from it. The farther we run the more we lose sight of what God really wants from and for us.

It is exactly at this point in the process when procrastination becomes dangerous: when it causes us to lose sight of what God wants, and so results in a pattern of disobedience. Without true obedience to God, we will lose our purpose and thus lose our peace.

This book is about such a man, a procrastinator whose refusal to follow God's desires cost him any sense of peace. His disobedience put not only himself, but also an entire city, in great danger. His name was Jonah.

Jonah is the practical role model of quite a few of us today. In fact, Jonah is the role model for a large portion of the Church of the United States of America. Let's face this: we've allowed ourselves to run from the voice of the Lord. The farther we try to run, the greater the sea rages around us.

America is in turmoil. Sin is a comfortable citizen within in our borders. Our transgression is full-grown and strong within our midst. As we approach the 21st century we must face some hard facts about our nation.

First, *as a nation we are divided on many issues*. At the recent Olympic games in Atlanta we all marveled at the efforts of athletes who had trained for countless hours. We cheered for those who came from every nation. Some of these athletes came from heart-wrenching poverty and war-torn strife. Their stories made us pause and wonder what would we do if we were put into such situations. The loudest cheers, however, were for the athletes who wore the red, white and blue of the United States of America. We collectively stuck out our chests as our athletes, from the Dream Team to the lady gymnasts, ran away with the medal count. By the sound of our cheers and the number of mini-flags waving, one would think the citizens of this rich nation were singing from the same hymn book.

Nothing could be further from the truth. From pro-life to pro-choice, pro-gun to Brady bill supporters, Democrat to Republican to Libertarian to Reform Party, we argue constantly. Our continuous bantering assures the talk shows long runs as we publicly air our dirty laundry.

Second, *we are still a nation that is divided over race.* "Race" has become the four-letter word of our generation. At one time it was believed by many that the issue was dead or dying. But it has become amazingly clear that for every step we took in the area of progress, we took at least two steps sideways. We never really got away from the problem; we just changed the angle.

The problem of racial division and hatred is not one that just affects blacks and whites. The entire nation takes a role in this morbid play that we act out on a daily basis from sea to shining sea. Native Americans, Latinos and Asians are also part of the theater that has turned the melting pot into the boiling pot. More times than not the main characters are black and white, the two most distant members of this ethnic rainbow.

Recent history has taught us much about ourselves. The O.J. Simpson verdict, which at the writing of this book is still a hot topic on nightly talk shows, caused a huge rip in the fabric of our flag. Blacks overwhelmingly thought the verdict was correct, given the directions of the judge and the evidence. Whites, on the other hand, felt the opposite in similar numbers. If things had ended with a few lively debates we could chalk it up to media hype and move on. Unfortunately the debate continues, and not in entirely civilized ways.

Black waitresses at restaurants and baggage handlers at airports have told me whites would allow them to serve them and not leave a tip. One baggage handler said he had several customers who allowed him to carry their bags, and instead of offering a tip they looked at him and said, "Not guilty."

As a child I heard the stories of church bombings, never thinking that I would personally see their like. Unfortunately churches are still burning today. The vast majority of these burnings happen to "black" churches in the south, much as it was thirty-plus years ago. The reaction of the public has been mixed at best, ranging from outcry to silence. Dollars have been raised to assist in the rebuilding of some of the churches; others have heard their last sermon. Majority white-attended churches have also been burned down. Because of some incidents of mostly-white member churches having been burned down, many are willing to minimize the torching of black churches. Still, history tells us that we all should be yelling from the rooftops instead of blaming pastors and congregations of insurance fraud.

That leads me to fact number three: *Sunday morning is still the most segregated time of the week.* Why? What's wrong with the Body of Christ? Why is it taking us so long to be unified? Do we really want to be reconciled? Is racial reconciliation what we're looking for anyway?

Many blacks have told me they are tired of trying the "racial reconciliation thing." "It's gotten old," one black man said. "I don't care if they love me or not. They're just trying to make themselves feel good anyway." But how do we preach 'the body' concept without practicing it? We can't fulfill the role of the church unless we love one another. Many whites tell me that all the affirmative action, equal rights, "I have a dream" talk simply doesn't meet them where they live. They say, "It's not my fault blacks were slaves in the first place. I wasn't alive then." Yet when it's time to celebrate a great victory or accomplishment of the past by whites, the same folks take great pride. It doesn't seem to matter that these things were accomplished long before their birth. Selective ownership is rampant in our land.

The division among Americans seems to be getting wider. While there have been significant strides toward equality, the hearts and minds of many Americans have not been affected. Worse still is the example the church has set. We should be known for our love and unity. Instead, we are undoubtedly known for almost everything *except* unity.

Much of our problem deals with what we feel about each other culturally. It's time for a change. Scripture says,

> *For it is time for judgment to begin with the family of God; and if it begins with us, what will the outcome be for those who do not obey the gospel of God? (1 Peter 4:17)*

Only four chapters in length, the book of Jonah speaks volumes about the human condition. It's the story of a man of God who fought a great war within himself. His war is a war that many of us fight today. While the church is indeed the beloved of God, we have become comfortable with our sin. One sin that distinguishes itself from the others has done more to turn people from the cross than any other. It's the same sin that drove Jonah away from God's call: racism.

The sin of racism is alive and well in the church today. Our minds and hearts are made up concerning some of those who look different than us. We've decided who we will love and who we will hate, often by the color of their skin. That sad fact has sent a terrible shock wave through our congregations. It has allowed heartache to visit our children and grandchildren. The strength of this great enemy has almost polarized us beyond repair.

Jonah's story also speaks of the love of his God; a love that has no boundaries, a love that reaches into the city while seeking to correct generations of wrong in one man's heart. Even after being rejected, God's love seeks to heal a second time. And as he did with Jonah, God is speaking to us a second time. As the modern-day Jonah, only the church can answer his voice. Will we procrastinate, run farther away, or heed his call?

Our happiness and peace within God's Kingdom depends on the decision we make. Our very survival into the next century hinges on our response to the word of God as he speaks to us again. The future of our children depends on the choice the Church makes in the upcoming months and years.

We can find ourselves in the story of Jonah. We can also find answers for the spirit that has possessed us far too long. It is an act of remarkable grace that God is allowing the church in America the opportunity to choose, for a second time in a generation, to truly be one in Christ. It is also an urgent responsibility. Procrastination has already put us in danger. The consequences of further disobedience are unthinkable.

Just ask Jonah.

Chapter One
Go to the City

The word of the Lord came to Jonah son of Amittai: "Go to the great city of Nineveh and preach against it, because its wickedness has come up before me." (Jonah 1:1,2)

Most of us have heard the story of Jonah and the whale. It's kind of the biblical "Jaws" story: the guy gets swallowed by the big fish.

It's too easy to take a look at Jonah in Sunday school and gloss over his experience. The tendency is to look at him as an example of what happens if we don't do what God asks us to do. That much is an accurate assessment, but the story of Jonah goes much further than that. Let's take a close look at this man and see what he has in common with us in the modern church.

When the Word Comes
The book of Jonah starts with a great phrase. "The word of the Lord came...." is used throughout scripture by other prophets as a mark of their calling. "The word of the Lord" was always coming to someone in the Old Testament, it seems. The first verses of the books of Hosea, Joel, Micah, Zephaniah, Haggai, and Zechariah all start with that same phrase. It's a clear indicator that, during those times, a prophet was deemed such not by any human ordination or by membership in the "prophet club," but by God himself. These were special men called for critical times -- and they weren't necessarily professional religious leaders. Consider the example of Amos:

> *Amos answered Amaziah, "I was neither a prophet nor a prophet's son, but I was a shepherd, and I also took care of sycamore-fig trees. But the Lord took me from tending the flock and said to me, "Go, prophesy to my people Israel." (Amos 7:14,15)*

Neither Amos, Isaiah nor Jeremiah were anxious to be prophets. Even in the middle of his ministry, Amos thought he didn't have enough formal prophet training. Isaiah thought he was too sinful to ever be used of God. Jeremiah believed he was just too young. But they all eventually responded to the desire of the Almighty God.

Here's the bottom line: when the word of the Lord comes to anyone, it's time to adjust your schedule. God chose individuals himself and commissioned them for his task. It's just the way God does business. The basis of the prophet's life is the confidence that God is able to communicate with humankind, making known to them his will. It is based more in "forthtelling" -- applying God's will to life today -- than in "foretelling" the future. (That isn't to say that forthtelling and foretelling exclude each other, mind you. Just watch the balance in the force of the message given to the biblical prophets, and you'll see what I mean.) Without the revelation of God there is no forthtelling message, and with no such message there can be no prophet.

The very fact that God is calling speaks against procrastination on the part of those called. The call of God is an invitation to *action* on the Word of God, which is his revealed will. God's commanding call must be answered, and answered with active obedience.

That's because God's call is irrevocably tied to his desire that his order in the universe be increased. There is a purpose in his call.

Order and Intervention

One more time: God's call is always tied to his purpose, and his purpose is to destroy sin before it destroys his children.

God's call is the means by which he makes people -- like you and me -- who are entirely unqualified into choice instruments of his will. That call will often lead to suffering for God's sake, because the powers and principalities set against God's purpose will do their utmost to neutralize God's agents who could bring the message of salvation to those drowning in sin.

Sometimes those attacks are overt. Sometimes they're not. Jonah's danger was not from the storm, or from the fish, or even from the Ninevites. His danger was that he might listen to the subtle voices that made his heart hard against the very city God was calling him to. His own prejudice could have thwarted his role as a prophet.

Subtle evil often combines with overt sin to produce a force so intense that it rises to God's attention and snaps his head around. That's the indication of the phrase "its (Nineveh's) wickedness has come up before me." If you thought God was just a cosmic mechanic who set the universe in order and has left us to our own devices, think again. God is ready and able to intervene in human affairs through judgment, and sin has been the red flag that has caught his attention from humankind's earliest history.

The intense kind of sin that is like that of Nineveh is referred to many times in scripture. Here are five examples for you to consider:

1) Cain's murder of his brother Abel: *The Lord said, "What have you done? Listen! Your brother's blood cries out to me from the ground." (Gen. 4:10)*
2) The evil of Noah's day: *Now the earth was corrupt in God's sight and was full of violence. God saw how corrupt*

Go to the City 11

the earth had become, for all the people of the earth had corrupted their ways. So God said to Noah, "I am going to put an end to all people, for the earth is filled with violence because of them." (Gen. 6:11-13)

3) Sodom and Gomorrah: *Then the Lord said, "The outcry against Sodom and Gomorrah is so great and their sin so grievous that I will go down and see if what they have done is as bad as the outcry that has reached me. If not, I will know." (Gen. 18:20,21)*

4) Babylon: *After this I saw another angel coming down from heaven. He had a great authority, and the earth was illuminated by his splendor. With a mighty voice he shouted: Fallen! Fallen is Babylon the Great! She has become a home for demons and a haunt for every unclean and detestable bird. For all the nations have drunk the maddening wines of her adulteries. The kings of the earth committed adultery with her and the merchants of the earth grew rich with her excessive luxuries. Then I heard another voice from heaven say: Come out of her, my people, so that you will not share in her sins, so that you will not receive any of her plagues; for her sins are piled up to heaven, and God has remembered her crimes. (Rev. 18:1-5)*

5) Nineveh: *The word of the Lord came to Jonah son of Ammitai: "Go to the great city of Nineveh and preach against it, because its wickedness has come up before me." (Jonah 1:1,2)*

Wickedness. Rampant sin. Judgment was about to fall in every situation above, because the degree of evil had become such a stench before God. God was about to personally intervene in human affairs because the nature of the sin was so reprehensible.

A closer look at our country might make you wonder what's keeping Him from intervening in America right now.

Here's a quick comparison of the sins that the Bible notes
will bring special attention from God against the societal
behavior of America today:

1. *The spilling of innocent blood.* Consider the impact of
abortion alone in this country – to the tune of 1.6 million
such procedures annually -- and how that alone must grieve
Jesus, who pointed to children as being examples in the
Kingdom of God.
2. *Excessive, senseless violence.* In recent years, the United
States has become a hands-down winner of the highest rating
for violence in the free industrialized world.
3. *The approval – and even encouragement – of
homosexual behavior.* From states considering the
endorsement of same-sex marriages to "Heather Has Two
Mommies" in public schools, the US is flying in the face of
biblical standards.
4. *Governments and economic systems that flaunt
immorality and excess.* The adulteries and moral failings of
our leaders bring about a national snicker instead of a call to
repent. Our hard hearts show in our treatment of the poor.
For example, some social scientists say that the US *throws
away* enough food each year to feed all the hungry nations of
the world.
5. *Racism.* It was a huge problem for Nineveh – and Jonah.
You don't think it's a problem anymore for America and the
church? Think again.

The Unspoken Apostasy
      I believe that God in years past chose the church of the
United States of America to be a prophet to the world.
He took immigrants from different lands and, despite their
meager beginnings, allowed them the opportunity to form a
nation that would be biblically based and led. Those who

made up the church of this new group were the voice of God to the people.

These pioneers grew as a nation and as a church. As they marked new territory they prayed, sang and preached every acre of the way. Lifting banners to God in each new area, the church of these United States learned the meaning of hard work and dedication. The work of faith was often an everyday part of life. As towns, farms and cities began to rise from the dust of the earth, this new nation found itself each Sunday morning on its knees. Often our best leaders were in the pulpits.

Many of the great hymns of the church were penned during these genesis years of the United States. Some of our more eloquent preachers traveled the land from one town to another spreading the faith. In many instances, the hope of the Word was all that stood between the settlers succeeding or failing. The church in America was growing and prospering. These new leaders were not the kings and queens from their motherland. On the contrary, many of them were outcasts and second class citizens. But God saw something in them. He caused them to defeat the armies of the land across the waters and settle into a new country where "all men are created equal."

At least we agreed to those words in principle. Almost from the beginning of our nation, something was wrong with part of this new church. When the new inhabitants of this great land began to grow and prosper, they began to show some traits of the countrymen they left behind in the Old World. They had brought some bad customs with them, one of which reared its head almost immediately.

That was the custom -- and sin -- of racial prejudice. This wrong was first condoned by the church when the slaughter of this country's original inhabitants began. Native Americans, mistakenly called "Indians," originally welcomed the settlers to this land of theirs with open arms.

They actually showed the immigrants from Europe how to survive the initial winters, which were very difficult. However, because of a lack of understanding of Native American culture, religion and customs, it was determined by many in the church that America's native people were just "savages." The situation deteriorated for years until many believed (and some preached) that "the only good Indian was a dead Indian."

The church's response? The very best scenario would be to help them to accept "our Jesus," as though Jesus could be owned and clearly identified in the mirror of any self-respecting Christian of European descent. That attachment to appearances drove missionaries to teach Native American converts to dress, talk, sing and act like "civilized people."

Too often, the Gospel became lost in that cultural shuffle, most of which was needless. The truth is that these were and are very civilized people. The Native American civilizations were different than civilizations in Europe, to be sure. The nations that had been established for centuries in Native America were indeed distinct from the society that was emerging as the United States -- but they were still viable civilizations that could have made this country and the church much stronger than they have become.

Native Americans are not alone as a people group alienated inside our country's borders. Asians, Hispanics and African American have often found themselves "on the other side of grace" in our society. Sadly, that alienation made its way quickly into the pews of God's appointed agent of grace: the church.

For years in our history, many of our nation's churches would not allow visitors of different races inside the four walls. Such a practice was considered undignified, or outright sin. Singing songs and reading scripture, those same godly forefathers who penned such eloquent words into some of our original laws and founding documents also authored documents and laws designating blacks as non-human property or, at best, three-fifths human.

God's Investment Means Responsibility

Much as God has invested in the church of the United States, God had invested much into Jonah. By the time of his call to preach against Nineveh Jonah was not a novice. He was not a one-time wonder. The name "Jonah son of Amittai" is also found in 2 Kings 14:25, and is used there in reference to Jonah's prophetic work in Israel -- a topic never really addressed in the book bearing his name. Jonah's ministry indeed went beyond his trouble dealing with his call to Nineveh. (This should prove that Jonah was a real person and not some character in a biblical parable. Jesus even spoke about him in Matthew 12: 30-41 as he gave an example of his death, burial and resurrection.)

Yes, Jonah was a chosen vessel of God to do a particular work in his generation. It seems that the work for which he is best remembered was only a high point in his career, and possibly a mission that was not well received among his own people: simply to go to the city of Nineveh and preach.

Nineveh was a city on the east bank of the Tigris River. Many historians believe it began as a Babylonian city, but most of Nineveh's history was as an Assyrian city, and eventually its capital. At the time of Jonah's ministry, Nineveh was "the great city" of Assyria. It was a large city that had become a large mess. The city was very wicked, brutal and immoral. Nineveh's claim to fame among its neighbors was that its citizens had developed very creative means of torturing prisoners, especially foreigners. The people of this metropolis felt they could live in whatever manner they wanted, and be accountable to no one. And God was calling Jonah to go and preach to them.

Isn't that just like God to call us to go into places we would probably rather avoid? Out of all the cities and towns in that region, God said to Jonah, "Go to Nineveh."

Some of us have been called to be prophets in our own personal Nineveh. It may be in a city that you would prefer to avoid, or a neighborhood frequently in the news because of a rising crime rate. Or, your Nineveh might simply be a group of people that just don't seem to be "your kind of folks."

As a church we have been part of the great migration. The majority of our citizens live within cities today. If we are not urban dwellers we're part of that fraternity known as "sub-urbanites."

As the Body of Christ it has been our mission to go to the city and preach against the evil that occurs there. The evils that are more commonly focused on are those that deal with overt, visible crime. We often speak of the violence and drugs. We spend hours discussing murder, teen pregnancy, and the other "buzz word" sins that politicians and preachers use to raise money and fear.

But there are other, more subtle evils in the city. Those are the ones we normally give attractive, acceptable names: "abortion," "embezzlement," "tax evasion" and "alternate sexual lifestyles." These "pretty sins" on the surface are still unrighteous to the core. God has called us to cry out against every form of evil.

We must cry out, not just for our sakes but for those who will follow us. We live in a society today that is largely the product of those who came before us. They planted the seeds; we're reaping the harvest. Think what you will, the good in the foundation laid by our forefathers is the reason for most of our current success. So we must make no mistake in our thinking: if we desire a better world for our children, then it will take an all-out effort to do the good God commands today.

God had given Jonah a clear word of judgment for the people: "Its wickedness has come up before me." Jonah's word for Nineveh was to be a definitive message from God. God wanted them to know that he saw their sin; in fact, the sin of Nineveh was directly in his face. The sight and the stench of their behavior was distasteful to him. But, even in the foul condition the society was in, God still found it within his grace to send the man of God to speak to them. Instead of a swift and complete destruction God called his messenger to give a word of warning.

Judgment was about to fall on Nineveh, and to the people of God, it was no mystery why. What was a mystery to Jonah was why God even wanted to bother to warn Nineveh. It was only mystery, though, because Jonah had to deal with sin of his own.

Judgment could be about to fall on America. It would be no mystery to most of the church. But we have the same problem of sin in our own house that Jonah had. It keeps us from being the prophet we must become as the church. And the very survival of our country depends on God's people dealing decisively with our own sins of pride and racism. Many of us trust God to judge the world today. Indeed, it *is* God's world to judge and not our own.

But why are we writing off our country in many instances without the Lord having to do anything with it? We're too quick to cry for judgment on those around us. How quickly we forget from whence we came. Not long ago we were sinners without a clue about how to escape from our habits and addictions. It's only by the grace of God that we now have this freedom, so misunderstood yet so envied by many still caught up in the world system.

How soon we forget that God, in his sovereign love, sent someone to rescue us. It wasn't because we deserved it, but because he loved us. His love is far beyond anything I can imagine.

My children are so dear to me. They're all different, yet they all make my heart glad. My son James is constantly asking for things. His vocabulary is quite developed for someone his age. He uses that "word power" to find ways to ask for information, gifts and favors almost constantly. His older brother Craig is just the opposite. He is quiet and very seldom asks for anything. (Most times my wife and I must check to see if Craig's still in the house.)

Though my sons are quite different, I love them just the same. Should one ever leave our home and decide to live a contrary lifestyle to what we desire, our love for that son will not change. My hope will always be that he return to the path we feel is more appropriate, but we will always love him.

God's love is so much more sophisticated than ours. His ability to love cannot be comprehended in our finite minds. Yet he uses us to draw some of his wayward children home. Sometimes we plant a seed. Other times we water the seed someone else plants. But always God is the one that causes it to grow and produce fruit.

God's wisdom is also much more sophisticated than ours. When we predetermine that we will not heed God's call to "go to the city" we say that we are wiser than almighty God. We tell him that our brother isn't important to us, and so should not be important to God. That attitude is rampant in the church in our country. We display it on a consistent basis. Except for token acts of fellowship, we seldom reach beyond our spheres of immediate, comfortable influence. The gospel has become a consoling pillow for our heads while millions around us drown in sin.

Where is the Church?

God instructed Jonah to go to a place that was accessible to him. While he needed some mode of transportation for the journey, his trip was well within reach for him. He was not asked to travel halfway around the world to get to these people.

It's the same for the church in America. While I am sure God has called many of us to support foreign missions, I am equally sure he has not called all of us to do so. It seems as though our country is in love with the idea of sending money or missionaries overseas. But what of the poor, hungry and hurting within our own borders? It has become a painfully common practice among evangelicals to blame the poor of this country for their poverty, and in the same breath take credit for the prosperity with which God has blessed us. Let's face this: if it had not been for God's grace toward our families, many of us would be in the same shape (or worse) than the poor we tend to criticize.

God calls us to go to those who are in need because he has qualified us to do so. Our education level is not what qualifies us; it is our level of experience with the Master that allows the words to proceed out of us that break the chains of sin. No other group of Americans can make the claim of having life in the words they speak. It is our lack of concern and love for those still in bondage that allows counterfeits to take our rightful place in the lives of those we could reach. The television screens of our country are filled with these false prophets. Since people are so desperate for an answer, and we are not willing to give them one, the false prophets have. Some are the "psychics and friends" who claim they want the troubled to be comforted. But the "forthtelling" message God gives his own demands dealing with present reality, not with dreaming of pie in the sky. How many paychecks will we let them waste to play the psychic's numbers to try to hit the lottery on a distant "someday?" How many relationships will we allow to die when, in our silence, men and women leave their families in search of their "ultimate soul mates?"

This phenomenon is yet another attempt by the enemy to rob the souls of humankind. But it doesn't stop there. Where is the church when people need compassionate moral guidance? Recent years have seen a marked decrease in prostitutes with the advent of the HIV/AIDS plague. Instead of the church uniting in an effort to comfort and rescue the millions of men and women who were looking for a solution to their addictions to sex, we stayed away and they found the higher-tech cultural alternative: phone sex lines.

Go down the shopping list of sin, pick any category that hurts our society, and then ask the tough question: *Where is the church? Are we running to answer God's call, or running away from it?*

We are called to the city -- Nineveh to so many of us -- because we are qualified to do what our government can't. We are called to the city because we are set apart to be salt and light of the world. We cannot expect God to call anyone else but us to do the job that must be done. We *are* the Jonahs of this generation. If we don't heed the call of God for us, our country is doomed.

And we will not be able to blame God, or the Nineveh around us.

Chapter Two
The Flight to Tarshish Heights

But Jonah ran away from the Lord and headed for Tarshish.
He went down to Joppa, where he found a ship bound for
that port. After paying the fare, he went aboard and sailed
for Tarshish to flee from the Lord. (Jonah 1:3)

This is a strange turn of events: Jonah -- the man of God ,
the prophet of God, the one in whom God entrusted "the
word" -- bailed out on God's call.

Apply Jonah's situation to yourself for a moment. Don't
you wish you had what Jonah had to set you apart from the
crowd: the God of the universe giving you specific personal
direction? Most Christians I know have this inner desire to
be someone to whom God communicates in a special way.

And don't you want to be a hero, especially in a society
of hero worshippers? The dictionary defines a hero as "a
person of distinguished valor; the person who has the
principal share in some exploit." We have a "hero fixation"
in this country. We pay millions of dollars each month to see
the latest movie hero blast through an entire army of enemies
alone.

There are other kinds of heroes than the kind we see too
often on the big screen, of course. Jonah was in the prime
position to become the hero and save this evil city, Nineveh,
from itself. But he refused. Maybe that's why we don't
generally consider Jonah to be one of the great Bible heroes.
(Too bad for Jonah; there's an entire book about him in the
scriptures. Maybe he needed a campaign manager.) It's just
that Jonah generally doesn't strike us as someone we pattern
ourselves after -- or do we?

Looking for the Reason to Run

Why did Jonah run from God?

People usually run from things because of fear. Was Jonah afraid of the people of Nineveh? The Bible does say that the city was full of wickedness. Could this wicked society have been filled with such evil that God's man feared for his own life or reputation if he entered its gates? It's a reasonable assumption based on the historical record. But it isn't backed up by any scriptural evidence about Jonah, who doesn't exactly come across as a shrinking violet when it was time to preach.

Maybe Jonah's reason for running stemmed from his low self-esteem. Many of us have been told that we don't measure up to someone else's standards, and for too many of us that becomes a serious problem. Could it be that Jonah compared himself to the other prophets of his time, and those who came before him, and reasoned that he didn't have "the right stuff" to carry off the task? I'm sure in Jonah's day, like ours, there were sufficient reasons to feel inadequate – the way you looked, the opinion you held, your lack of social graces. We are constantly reminded that our society believes some people are better than others. (Personally, I have been counted with the "others" more than I would like.) But God has a unique way of bolstering the confidence of his messengers, even if we only tap into that faith for particular tasks, so looks and social status really don't matter. While Jonah had a unique situation before him, there's really no indication that he had a self-esteem problem, or even a lack of confidence.

Another reason we run from tasks we should take on is lack of preparation. Maybe Jonah found himself unprepared to preach the kind of message God had charged him to carry to Nineveh. I know in my early years of ministry there were days when I stood to preach or teach and felt totally unprepared for the task. I wasn't afraid to face the people, I just felt I didn't have the correct words to get the message across. Like most of you, I had heard great orators wax eloquently from the pulpit. They can take ordinary words and make them dance like a ballet company. My words do well just to walk on stage. (Of course, there are those who don't mind boring people to death or -- worse -- giving an inappropriate message in critical times. The truth is they *should* mind.)

Once Pastor Willie Vaughn of Kansas City told me a parable of two shepherds. One was old, the other young. The young shepherd had a good flock, and was even beginning to get a reputation as a successful shepherd. He couldn't help but notice, though, that the older man's flock was remarkably obedient -- and so much more than his own sheep that he determined to ask his older friend for advice.

"Sir, what's your secret? Sometimes I have to call my flock until my throat is hoarse before they come. Your sheep come to you immediately when you call just once. How do you do it?"

The old shepherd bent down and picked up a bucket full of feed. He answered the question by calling his sheep. While they were coming to him, he busied himself filling their feed troughs. He looked up at his younger friend and smiled as he said, "I never call my sheep unless I have something to feed them."

Wouldn't it be wonderful if the same should be said about ministers of the Gospel? When we call our flocks together they should expect a full nourishing meal from God's Word, instead of some warmed over, stale, non-digestible, canned group of words we pull together from our own finite minds.

But God himself had spoken to Jonah. He had given his prophet the word for that time. We simply can't say that Jonah was unprepared.

The entire story of Jonah from beginning to end is that of a man called to be a prophet, but stubbornly refusing to accept his commission. We know that Jonah wasn't afraid of the people. Every indication is that he was prepared and had enough confidence for the task. But for some reason, this apparently able individual decided to run from the Lord. *Why then did he run?*

"Just Say 'No'" and a Contest of Wills

What we have here is a contest of wills: God's will versus Jonah's will. Defined as a verb, "will" means "to determine by choice." Jonah's choice regarding Nineveh and its inhabitants was the opposite of God's choice. God wanted Nineveh to have the chance to feel his mercy, not just his judgment. God had appointed Jonah to speak on his behalf to Nineveh so the great city could choose to repent.

And there entered the contest of wills. Jonah had no problem with pronouncing judgment. As a matter of fact, he longed for Nineveh to be judged. Jonah's problem was what he knew about God's mercy. God indeed was, and is, a God of mercy. Time and again, Scripture indicates God's mercy toward humankind after a pronouncement of well-earned judgment. Jonah was aware of God's character, and so was aware of his mercy.

The issue became who controlled God's mercy. The biblical answer is self-evident. In Exodus 33:19 and Romans 9:15 the decision is placed squarely with God:

"I will have mercy on whom I have mercy, and I will have compassion on whom I will have compassion."

That only makes sense. The choice for mercy is clearly the Lord's, but Jonah felt Nineveh didn't deserve any choice in the matter, even *God's* choice. And he wasn't about to give God a chance to exercise his right to show mercy.

The people of Nineveh were no strangers to Jonah. It is a good assumption that the Assyrians were the most hated of any of Israel's enemies at the time. Jonah knew of their escapades and victories over his people. Because of the times his people were overrun by the Assyrians and even deported, Jonah had a deep hatred for Nineveh.

So we arrive at the cause of Jonah's disobedience. It has nothing to do with fear, confidence or lack of preparation. His motive is simple hatred of the people of Nineveh. Jonah was prejudiced against Nineveh because of the history between his people and those who lived in that city. For Jonah, the possibility of "those people" sharing in the privileges of Israel was unthinkable. Even though he had done great things for God, Jonah allowed his prejudice to keep him from God's call on his life. God had uniquely prepared Jonah to be a hero -- to give God's word to people God had determined were ready to receive it -- and Jonah chose to play God. He just said, "No. They don't deserve the word of God, much less his mercy."

The Wrong Time to Just Say "No"

Let's face this: the church in America has a history of running from the Lord, too.

We've had no problem protecting the borders of our nation against enemies real, created or imagined. We've fought brilliantly and faithfully when we think our freedoms are being threatened. The support of the church of Jesus Christ has been welcomed and appreciated by presidents and generals alike during times of national crisis. From the crash of Wall Street to the conflict of Desert Storm, the church has been a crucial part of the victories and the post-crisis healing we've experienced in this nation. Our legacy as a body in the United States is well-documented. While we've faced some persecution now and then, there is no doubt this country has treated the church with honor and respect.

The same cannot be said about how we, the church in the United States, treat our fellow Americans (or even our fellow members of the body of Christ). The church in this country has, in many cases, been more hostile to our own family than the world has. We've given "The Big Four" -- Class, Culture, Color and Church Denomination -- free rein to divide us. These four categories of division have neutered much of the effectiveness the church could have had in our generation.

Still, the one category that has hurt our efforts the most is the "race card." While the American church has had some role in progressive race relations over the years, it has had a larger role in racial division. Consider the church and the slavery issue. We are aware that, years ago, many of our church leaders owned slaves themselves. But what's worse is our insistence on maintaining the status quo in function after the slaves were legally free. We are aware that some of our most respected denominations formally ruled that race separation was mandated by God. But why, long after it was abolished, has the American church largely maintained a "pew length" distance from those of different races and cultures? For more years than I've been alive, the saying "Sunday morning is the most segregated time of the week" has been, and is still, true.

The church has let its fear, lack of preparation, lack of cultural understanding and bigotry move us from our call. Like Jonah, we have run from God when he asked us to show mercy to a people in need of His word. Jonah disguised his bigotry as a desire for "justice" for past transgressions against his people. The church today feels justified as it avoids issues of justice for the people we simply don't care for.

Through the lenses of conservatism we have watched and listened as countless numbers of pastors, teachers and laymen call for the return of the "good old days." But for whom were those days good, anyway? Certainly not for the millions of Native Americans who were killed, raped and cheated out of their land and dignity. Certainly not for the countless numbers of African Americans who were enslaved, stripped of their pride, culture, language, name, history and rights. Even in the 20th century, the 40s and 50s (the "good old days" for a lot of us) were a time with laws that wouldn't let many of us play on the same ball fields together, much less vote.

During the height of the civil rights movement blacks, in prayerful protest and dignity, petitioned the evangelical church to join them in the struggle for right. That part of Christ's body stayed on the sidelines, for the most part. The reason? Civil rights leaders were supposedly involved with "suspicious characters." Then the race laws began to fall and it was legal for all of God's children to come together. It was finally legal to sing, preach, learn, play and even live together. How did the church in America respond? Instead of coming together in the mid-to-late 60s and exhibit the kind of family only the church can, the majority church ran from the city. Instead of staying and working with other members of the same body, the church took off with the rest of the world. It took the same stance as millions of other former urbanites and fled to the suburbs: Tarshish Heights.

What Are We Afraid Of, Anyway?

Why did we run? More importantly, why do we continue to run? Could it be that the those who are part of this vast population are afraid? And if so -- *afraid of what?* Crime rates? It's true the crime picture for many cities of America is bleak, but it's also true that cities have always been relatively unsafe. It's this simple: where there are large groups of economically deprived people, crime usually follows.

I've had my share of experiences from the hands of the criminal element, from robberies to murders. But it has been my experience that crime in this country has absolutely nothing to do with the color of someone. It has more to do

with the heart and mind of the individual. The inner
workings of a man or woman has more to do with their
behavior than the hue of their skin.

Given that, who is more able to help in the shaping of an
individual than the church? What organization did the Lord
command to assist those who were less fortunate? Which
group was charged to encourage children to come to the Lord
Jesus? Wasn't the same group given the challenge of going
into all the world to make disciples? Nowhere in all of these
requests did God say to His people, "You are the underdog.
So guard your place in society and bend to its pressures."

Fear is a strange master. There is this 'fear' thing that I
have to always overcome when I'm traveling around the
country. It doesn't matter if I'm in a store or in a church; the
same thing usually happens. It's the kind of fear most of my
white brothers and sisters don't realize exists. It is a two-
edged sword.

On the one hand, some people fear me. When many
whites see me coming toward them they immediately change
their course. If I walk into a store aisle, people begin to move
-- usually quickly. If I come into a public washroom, guys
grab their briefcases and make a hasty exit. (Usually without
washing their hands...) If, as I walk, my path takes me close
to children parents panic and quickly grab the hands of their
child. (When I pass by, I often look back and notice how
things go back to normal after the 'black cloud' has passed.)
Little old ladies clutch their purses like a fullback headed for
the goal line. Security guards routinely follow me around
stores and those who have pledged to serve and protect stop
and frisk me instead.

I'm not feared because of my police record. I don't have
one. I'm treated like a rapist or a robber, but not because I
was acquitted due to lack of evidence. Most times it is
simply because of my color. Ask any of my white friends
who have been with me and watched the "black cloud"

phenomenon at work. They're amazed when it happens, and tell the stories better than I.

It's true there are far too many black criminals in our prisons, jails and on our streets. But there are plenty of white criminals, too. The truth is that most black men, regardless of their proven character, are looked upon as potential criminals. That sorry state of reasoning comes from lack of relationships and too much television.

I must admit, however, that sometimes it's better to be feared than hated. Hate is simply another side of fear that I constantly have to face. Recently I heard on the news that one out of every seven drivers in this country carries a gun. If that's true, I'm one of the six who is "gunless." Every so often as I'm driving, I find myself wondering, "What if someone driving alongside me has a gun? Which one is paranoid enough to shoot me if he thinks I'm looking at him too hard?" But it doesn't end there. Sometimes as I'm headed up the sidewalk toward a friend's new house I think, "What if I knock on the wrong door and someone thinks I'm trying to rob them?"

Were we even thinking that kind of "what ifs" a generation ago? The attitude and demeanor of our land has changed dramatically in the last 40 years. We've all identified closely with our own cultures, so we should feel more secure about our self-identities, right? So why does it seem like there's more hate across the lines now? We see and hear so much about gangs and the senseless violence they perpetrate, *but we seldom openly discuss the hate we generate in our own racial groups.*

Who do you think modeled hate for this generation? As a nation we applaud violence on the big screen. We even award it when it fascinates us. We teach our children that killing is wrong – unless it serves our purposes. Because of the size and wickedness of the hate in our land, it's very difficult to trust anyone anymore. We have so stigmatized and stereotyped one another that we just don't trust each other. Everybody has an enemy and none of us takes much responsibility for our own demise; it's all the other guy's fault. We've allowed the paranoid voices of radio talk show hosts to enlarge our fear of each other like a malignant tumor.

The world's fear of itself is bad enough. Fear has become the fastest growing fad in the nation. You can become a millionaire or a hero if you can convince enough people to fear another group.

What's worse, however, is the mindless way the church has followed suit. Yes, we've become an even greater example of this "Hurry! Let's get away from THEM!" cult. Consider what we label "Christian" radio and television. It can be sickening. Granted, some of these brothers and sisters in broadcasting tell the truth, and a few of them are actually quite interesting. But the endless shows that group poor children, single mothers and those who are caught up in sin into one tidy punching bag are shameful. Don't get me wrong: I believe that sin is transgression of God's law. In fact, that very belief drives me to question whether, on many occasions, whether those doing the finger pointing are bigger sinners than those they point out. Do they really have a more godly lifestyle than those on whom they focus? Much of what we call "righteous anger" is no more than warmed-over conservative political highbrow arrogance.

When we allow conservative "hatred harlots" or liberal "poverty pimps" to develop church policy or preaching, we prostitute the Gospel of Jesus Christ. We've sold ourselves out to those who would use us for their own gain.

What makes all this talk about fear into a tragedy is that fear -- save for a biblical fear of God -- should have no real hold on the American church. How can a group who truly has the ear of God be afraid? The answer is simple: they can't.

So are we afraid that somehow, we've lost God's favor?

In the same vein, how can a community which has control of the vast majority of wealth truly fear those who have relatively little? The answer again is quite simple: they can't. Unless, of course, they are unprepared to assist those who need assistance.

But is that the history of the church in America? As far as I can tell, that *can't* be the case. The American church has helped build the Body of Christ in every nation we've wanted to outside the United States. We've sent missionaries into every land we could find. Even when they didn't want us around anymore, we sent missionaries. Our churches and denominations have had decades to create curriculum and training to teach the Gospel to nations around the world. We entered these nations and lived among those people.

Why, then, do we refuse to live in the same community with those whom we share citizenship? We've educated and reeducated more teachers, preachers and evangelists than any other nation before us, so we really can't say we're unprepared.

The conclusion is painfully clear. Like Jonah, the church in this country has a hatred for some people. That hatred gives birth to a mindset that it is simply not fair for "those people" to share the same blessings they and their families enjoy.

The Mission at Home

The reasoning of the American church may not match Jonah's, but the result of their actions do.

Too often our home-directed missiology says people of various colors and cultures need Jesus, but not really anything else. We evangelicals will too often argue that "those people" just need Jesus. Here's an example: just give those kids in the inner city Jesus, and they'll be fine. But if that's the case, why do our children and families need training, finances, education, investment counseling and a host of other things that are never mentioned when we discuss "those other people?" We sing about the same God. We pray to the same God. Why can't we let Him convince us to live together beyond racial barriers? We've called upon a common Savior. Why can't we share our communities and churches? Why does our practical testimony have to say, "'Those people' just don't deserve to have the same things as 'normal folk.'"

God has spoken to the American church, just as He did to Jonah, to go to the city and preach against it. But our prophetic example must be to stay in the city and show the world an example of God's grace.

I truly believe God has and always had strong, genuine, faithful, powerful men and women of color in the city. And by no means am I suggesting that God couldn't move in the city without white Christians there. He has proven he can, time after time. Still, the body of Christ is one body made up of various members, *and God has never sent half a prophet to do a whole prophet's job.*

Each group brings various gifts to the other. If we so choose, we could form a great army that no enemy could stand against. Instead, we have separated ourselves and become weak and pitiful in the things that truly matter. Our token attempts at reconciliation and unity are a mockery to the call God has truly placed on our generation.

We should cry against any world system that would teach us to separate ourselves and discriminate against one another. God has called us to teach our children to love and respect other cultures in Christ. "Be my example in the world," Jesus said to us. "Be salt. Be light. Make a difference." But the church, like Jonah, has run from the Lord.

Jonah went to Joppa and found a ship that would take him away from where God had commanded him to go. Jonah said "no" to God's plan and chose to take a ship that would transport him away from God's chosen destination. He knew he was still God's prophet. He just didn't share God's desire to bless others different than himself.

Like Jonah, the church has found ways to transport us as far away from the city as we could get. "The neighborhood's changing." "They're not like us." "I can't have my children associating with *those* people." We used any excuse possible to abandon our houses of worship -- and our own homes -- in the city and started new communities known as suburbs. We've chosen the name "suburbanites," meaning "inferior to urbanites."

That would be great if we really took on the attitude that the name suggests, and counted ourselves as servants to those who minister in the Nineveh we refuse to face. But you and I know better, don't we?

Chapter Three
Against the Wind

Then the Lord sent a great wind on the sea, and such a violent storm arose that the ship threatened to break up. (Jonah 1:4)

Something happens to human beings when we make up our minds. We become like donkeys: bound and determined that we won't move.

The stubbornness of humankind is well documented. But the stubbornness of God's people is unique, because we can hear the voice of the Lord, get strong and straight direction, and still refuse to budge. Jonah is a prime example of that. Jonah's mind was made up. Jonah 1:3 recounts that, having decided to run from the Lord, he went to Joppa, found a ship bound for Tarshish, paid the fare, went aboard and sailed for Tarshish. Remember now, Jonah did all this to "flee from the Lord."

If we look at the phrase in context we notice that the man of God was not just running from the word of the Lord and the people in the city, but also from the Lord himself. Jonah thought he could actually get away from God by moving away from the place God had spoken to him. In the ancient Near East, people believed that a god virtually inhabited the area where his worshipers lived. In 2 Kings 5:17, for example, Naaman requests some soil from the place from which he was healed from leprosy. His thinking was that the land was holy and so had some sort of healing power.

What Naaman and Jonah alike failed to understand was that the entire earth belongs to God. But what about us? Could it be true, enlightened as we are today, that many of us avoid certain neighborhoods -- or people -- to stay away from God or his voice? Do we think that if we aren't around "those people" in "those places" that God won't speak to us about them?

Paying for Our Prejudice
    It's amazing how often we allow our prejudices, much less our preferences, to map out our life's course. Our prejudice has moved many of us far away from God's course and purpose for our lives. We talk a great fight. We say we're motivated by love to reach out to a hurting and dying world, but the reality is that many of us have been motivated by preference to reach out in our comfort zones. Our missionary giving in funds and time is strictly determined by our perception of who deserves it. God's desire for us is often lost in our desire, and that means the people in whom God would work redemption are often left wanting.
    Prejudice simply means "bias." We all have some prejudice. I am personally prejudiced against pumpkin pie. In fact, I hate the stuff. Many of my friends and family feel the same way about this traditional holiday cuisine simply because we prefer sweet potato pie. (Trust me: stacked up against sweet potato pie, pumpkin pie is just a poor substitute.) Having said that, know that my upbringing and culture sway my taste. My grandmother (and every other relative I know) would always prepare sweet potato pie during the holidays.
    Obviously, prejudice can be acquired from one's surroundings. Still, prejudice should not turn into racism, classism or any other "ism" that would separate us from God's will as it did for the prophet. Think about this: Jonah so disliked the people of Nineveh that he paid to get away from them. He parted with his hard-earned shekels to leave the area to which God was telling him to preach. Scripture doesn't indicate how much this cruise set Jonah back, but it *is* interesting to note that he wanted out so bad that he was

willing to pay for it. His mind was so made up to get away
that the cost was of no consequence to him.

In like manner, many of us have paid countless dollars to
get our churches and families away from the city. While
some Christians have made their presence known in the city
even after our exodus into suburban communities, there are
still thousands of us who left to be separate from "those
people" who were moving into "the hood."

The results? Not only did we pay untold millions to leave
the communities we had settled, but we forfeited even more
by often selling homes and churches for much less than they
were really worth. Greedy real estate agents gained the
advantage over scared owners who thought they would be
left behind in a neighborhood of "those people" if they didn't
hurry and sell. Because very few Christians ever stayed
around long enough to see if the new people were civil or
not, they sacrificed everything -- including potential
relationships -- out of fear. The fear proved to be not of the
people alone, but of communing with "those people" as
though they inferior and could taint (or worse, marry into)
their families.

"Those People" Are Here! (We're Leaving...)

My in-laws, the Dandridges, tell an interesting story
about their move into an almost-all-white community in
Chicago in the early 60s. Predictably, when they moved in
the "For Sale" signs started popping up almost immediately.
There were no Welcome Wagons or cookies from the
neighbors for my wife's family. Instead, real estate agents
spread panic through the block like wildfire: "The property
value's going down because the colored people are moving
in!" Their white neighbors believed the realtors and sold
their houses as quickly as they could. They didn't even ask if
the Dandridges were drug dealers, pimps or professors; they
just wanted out.

My future father in-law's next door neighbor was kind enough to strike up a conversation one day, though. He said "This is a good block. We understand your people's desires and ways. Just remember, when you eat your watermelon we don't like the seeds spit out into the street." Mr. Dandridge then replied, "We don't like to see watermelon seeds in the street either." He went on to explain to the startled neighbor that what he had heard was just a stereotypical tale about blacks. He told him that his wife was a school teacher, he was a postal worker and they were both Christians with small children. While this was enlightening to that neighbor, it didn't stop the white flight from my in-laws' block. It didn't matter if the blacks were Christian or sinner, professionals or welfare recipients. They were "those people" and had to be avoided at all costs.

Please understand that God is not in opposition to people living in different communities. He is, however, in opposition to people resisting his desire of brothers and sisters loving one another unconditionally. And how can you demonstrate unconditional love when you refuse to associate with those brothers and sisters?

Against the Wind

As Jonah boarded the ship, I imagine he felt he was on his way to a quieter existence. In fact, I'm sure he thought that things were going to go his way. Maybe he was even humming "Zip-a-Dee-Doo-Dah" on his way up the gangplank. Why *wouldn't* everything be going his way now? After all, he *was* escaping the presence of God – not to mention "those people." All he had to do now was travel to his destination, where he could celebrate the end of the journey and relax in a more peaceful environment.

But God had other plans for Jonah. In verse 4 of chapter 1 we read, "Then the Lord sent a great wind on the sea, and such a violent storm arose that the ship threatened to break

up." Jonah was traveling against the wind of God himself.
The Lord himself sent the great wind; this was no accidental
occurrence of nature. God's target for the wind was Jonah.
But the ship and everyone else on it were buffeted by that
same wind -- all because of Jonah's disobedience.

God chose to send that wind, as is well within his right
and power. Psalm 135: 5-7 confirms his might and the
witness of nature to it:

> *I know that the Lord is great, that our Lord is greater*
> *than all gods. The Lord does whatever pleases him, in*
> *the heavens and on the earth, in the seas and all their*
> *depths. He makes clouds rise from the ends of the earth;*
> *he sends lightning with the rain and brings out the wind*
> *from his storehouse.*

This vicious gust against Jonah and his fellow travelers
was indeed from the storehouse of God himself.

While God gives us the ability to make our own choices,
he also reserves the right to make choices of his own. The
Bible is packed full of examples of individuals whose
choices led them to disaster, from Cain and Korah to Judas
Iscariot and Herod. Yet there are other examples of
disobedient people who met God's intervention and turned
back to him. One obvious example is King David, who made
a series of disastrous choices out of lust for Bathsheba that
led him into conspiracy to murder, deceit, and adultery. But
when God sent the prophet Nathan to confront David, the
shepherd-king's heart was broken. He repented, and drew
close to God again -- much sadder, yet wiser.

Many of us have had personal experience with the wise
Father in heaven who has used his unseen wind to redirect
our steps. He has sent his precious Spirit to not only comfort
us but also to direct us in the way we should go. In Acts
2:1,2 the Bible says,

> *When the day of Pentecost came, they were all*
> *together in one place. Suddenly a sound like the blowing*

of a violent wind came from heaven and filled the whole house where they were sitting.

As the early church responded to the wind of God, they became God's agent of grace and change to the entire Roman Empire and beyond. But they had to learn not to travel against that wind.

When the Wind's in Your Face, Turn Around

Today I hear the wind of the Spirit blowing again. The message for the church today reaches past the early church to the journey of Jonah. God's saying, "Turn around."

Jonah was still God's man. He still had the title "Prophet of God" on his business card. Still, because of his disobedience to the voice and will of God he caused the wind to blow in direct opposition to his course. God is truly inescapable. Scripture puts it this way in Psalm 139:7-12:

Where can I go from your Spirit? Where can I flee from your presence? If I go up to the heavens, you are there; if I make my bed in the depths, you are there. If I rise on the wings of the dawn, if I settle on the far side of the sea, even there your hand will guide me, your right hand will hold me. If I say, 'Surely the darkness will hide me and the light become night around me,' even the darkness will not be dark to you; the night will shine like the day, for darkness is as light to you."

So here's what we must understand today: Jonah couldn't run from the presence of the Lord -- *and neither can the Church*. It doesn't matter how unsettling God's will may appear to us. What God commands us to do is truly a privilege. Our obedience is the way we show our love and trust in him. When we find our desires don't match his will, God has both the right and the means to call us to change our direction with this promise: he will never leave or forsake us. Neither will his word for us.

Reactions to the Storm: Past and Present

The storm's effect it on both the ship and her crew are intriguing. Verse 4 continues, ".... and such a violent storm arose that the ship threatened to break up." The literal meaning of the phrase "threatened to break up" is "thought it would break up." It's as though the ship itself was reacting to the storm in fear. Think about it: this ship was designed to perform in water. It was designer-built to dance across the waves under any circumstances. The last thing that should intimidate a boat is water, but this rough sea with its violent gale was even too much for Jonah's getaway vessel.

The story continues in verse 5: "All the sailors were afraid...." Not only was the boat quaking, the sailors too were terrified by the magnitude of the storm. The crew for this vessel were experts at their task. They were not novices who had never been on water before. No doubt they had seen countless storms and had navigated through them as a matter of routine. However, on this occasion the scene was vastly different. What was wrong? Why were these maritime experts trembling in fear? This wasn't just a matter of a couple of fearful sailors losing there nerve. To the contrary, "all the sailors were afraid." The fear was a result of the unusual fierceness of the storm on the water.

Many times water represents those things we can see and touch but can't control. In the Bible, water also represents obstacles that take supernatural faith or intervention to overcome. This was a case in which the turbulence on the water was caused by God's wind, and it disturbed even those who were trained to maneuver through it.

What is particularly interesting about our current storm is that the fierceness of the activity around us while the wind of God is in our faces. Our religious community seems to be rocking back and forth with an unusual vengeance in our chosen vessels of departure. While we are still the beloved children of the most high God, yet we are nonetheless in the midst of the most terrifying storm in recent history. The ships we sail -- industry, government, religion, politics -- looked very dependable, perhaps even respectable, when we first got on board. But now they seem destined to crash under the pressure of the storm.

Further, our chosen experts (not unlike the mariners of Jonah's time) are admitting that the storm we face goes beyond their abilities to navigate. For years we've looked to the experts on the sea of life to tell us everything from how to grow hair to how to lose weight. With such an abundance of expertise available on our bookshelves we should have control of all of life's situations, shouldn't we?

But the times we are living in are no ordinary seasons of minutes, days, weeks and months. For the first time in my life, I've heard experts put their rhetoric aside and confess they really don't have the answers to the problems that have arisen. From the AIDS crisis to the war on drugs, our "gurus of how-to" have reluctantly admitted in many cases they have no real answers. The government has gone from its "Just Say No!" campaign to building more prisons and digging more graves. The advice for our young people has gone from "Save yourself for marriage" to "Here's your condom."

"Church experts" have also shot some big blanks in the past few years. From the traditionalists to the charismatics we've seen revival services with no revival and healing lines without a cure. The "Word Movement" folks have "named it and claimed it" without very much success. In fact, they've named it and renamed it, married it and given it their surname, divorced it and given it nicknames. It's still nothing but a dance card with all the names crossed off. We've had enough conventions, collections, convocations and concerts to drive every devil back into hell months ago. Yes, God's Word is still the same. It will never change. We still see the sinner coming to cross with the success of salvation as the result. But aren't we just fooling ourselves if we don't take a hard look at all the gimmicks and games, designed to draw the crowds to our churches, conventions and concerts, that have been added to the grace of God for this generation?

The Featured Deity from Our Menu (?)

It is also interesting to note that *"each* (sailor) *cried out to his own god."* These men were obviously not upstanding Hebrews because they are mentioned in the context of calling out to their own gods. They must have had some sort of religious mind given that reaction when they realized they were in danger. Perhaps the sailors on Jonah's boat were not endowed with true faith, but at least they held some sense of dependence on a "higher power," in twelve-step language.

That futile dependence still holds in our misguided generation of experts. At the first sign of trouble around us, the word goes out to pray to whatever you choose as an object of faith. You can burn candles, gaze into crystals, or dial a 900 number. It doesn't matter to the experts. We have dozens of religions today; some old, some weeks old. It may comfort us that so many people have some sort of faith.

There's no question the constitution of our nation gives us certain rights, including the freedom to worship who or what we please. I thank God for that freedom. But there is evidence that we worship independence itself. For example, we're so independent in this country that we seem to crave our own gods as well. We don't question the track records of our chosen deities. That has no consequence on our trust in them. No doubt many of us are between gods now, like a teen between steady dates.

The fifth verse of the first chapter of Jonah concludes with the phrase, "...and they threw the cargo into the sea to lighten the ship." After their prayer session concluded, the sea was still tossing the boat like a rag doll. So the sailors decided on their back-up plan, and began to lighten the load of the ship. This was not brain surgery; the process was quite simple. It was the duty of the crew to take the tackles and other equipment along with some of the cargo and throw it into the water. This sacrifice of goods and equipment allowed the lighter ship to ride higher in the water, and so minimized the chances of the ship capsizing. The sailors realized that self-preservation was of more importance than the chance for greater profit, much less those items that were easily replaced at the next dock.

Our crew of experts are not so different. They'll turn to their gods only as long as it takes to realize those gods just aren't listening. The gods of religion, wealth, and even power are usually shunned when the wind keeps blowing. "Plan 2" (the backup plan) generally includes lightening the load. From downsizing a company to dumping a husband, wife or significant other, self-preservation is the key. The rule is, "If I can lighten the load, I have a better chance of riding out the storm." Like the sailors on the boat, our tendency is to believe that it's easier to pick up new supplies at the next dock in our lives.

But at what cost?

Chapter Four
How Can You Sleep?

But Jonah had gone below deck, where he lay down and fell into a deep sleep. The captain went to him and said, "How can you sleep?" (Jonah 1:5,6)

Actor Geoffrey Holder once said, "Sleep when you earn it."

Apparently Jonah wasn't one who lived by that creed. There's no doubt this had been a challenging day for the prophet. He'd started with a major disagreement with God. Then he ran away from God's appointed mission. He'd secured a ticket and become familiar with this getaway boat. Then a storm blew into the picture. Perhaps Jonah was thinking, "So what else could happen?" as he shrugged his shoulders and went below deck for a nap.

How interesting it is that a man with enough sensitivity to be a prophet of God became so insensitive to the events occurring around him.

How Can You Sleep?

One would imagine that Jonah might go below deck and pray that God have mercy on him for disputing the Almighty's plan. Perhaps Jonah would seek some quiet time for reflection on his actions, and possibly repent for his hasty decision. Unfortunately, Jonah's motives for going down into the hole of the ship weren't that noble. He just wanted to get some sleep.

Maybe he was tired from all the unplanned running. It was possible he just wanted to sleep through part of the long trip to hasten its end. Whatever the reason, as the vessel of disobedience pulls farther away from the land God wanted to show mercy, Jonah slipped deeper into dreamland.

The dictionary describes "sleep" as follows: "To take rest by a suspension of voluntary exercise of the power of body and mind; to be dormant or inactive." While Jonah was suspending the power of his body and mind, a severe storm arose on the sea. As mentioned in the previous chapter, God initiated this storm because of Jonah's disobedience to him. But Jonah was in such a deep state of sleep that he was unaware of the events around him. The waves banged against the sides of the ship, the vessel reeled from the force of the storm -- and Jonah slept through all the noise as well as the hurried actions of the sailors.

Then the captain of the ship went searching for the one member of his vessel who was missing. Maybe he thought the man who had paid to board his ship had been injured early in the storm. In all the rush and excitement, perhaps his passenger had even been washed overboard. Jonah was not with the rest of the crew, and the captain had a duty to make sure all those on board were safe. So he went into the lower portion of the ship and looked around. There was Jonah.

The Bible doesn't say how the ship's captain knew Jonah was sleeping and not injured. Maybe Jonah was curled up on some blankets with a nice smile on his face. Perhaps he was snoring so loud that he could be heard over the storm. Whatever the situation, the captain was not pleased at his slumber. He marched over to Jonah, awakened him and asked the first of two very intriguing questions the disobedient prophet must answer this day.

"How can you sleep?" The captain jolts Jonah to consciousness with an embarrassing query. His question comes from sheer amazement that a man could sleep so soundly in the midst of such a devastating storm. The events were shaking the boat and all those who were upon it, and this man had not even stirred. How could anyone sleep through such rough waters?

No doubt Jonah was coming to his senses and felt the boat shifting all around him. As his head cleared, the captain's question made more sense. The prophet probably felt confident in the knowledge that he was the man of God on the boat. He probably always slept well knowing that he was one of God's chosen vessels. Even in disobedience he felt safe enough to sleep soundly.

Slipping Deeper into Dreamland

How deep is our sleep in the current-day storm? There's no doubt we've scarcely seen such turmoil and travail in recent memory. Our country is being rocked back and forth with waves of crisis. From illegal drugs to violence of all sorts, we just can't keep the ship of our disobedience straight in the water. Our newspapers are filled with financial crises and reports on the breakdown of the family structure. "Alternative lifestyles" are being forced on our children in the guise of civil rights.

According to *The State of America's Children Yearbook 1996* (Children's Defense Fund, 1996), every day in America 2,883 children drop out of school. Daily, 1,407 teenagers give birth each day and 6,024 teens are arrested.

And the answers we hear from our political leaders? Build more prisons and give them condoms.

The storm keeps raging without any evidence of it subsiding soon. And when the question "Where's the church?" is asked, more often than we'd like to admit the answer is, "Sleeping."

Please don't look at this as an indictment on the entire Body of Christ. There are many fellowships and individuals who spend time, money and prayer to address the problems of the day. The church actively prevents many problems through the efforts of those who intervene in the lives of those who need help. We often read about such heroes in magazines and books that chronicle there deeds. Praise the Lord for those who follow the call of God on their lives without compromise, but could it be the reason for much of our celebration of them in the media is the lack of quality examples of true discipleship?

The fewer the examples, you see, the better the copy and video opportunities. We often enjoy the warm fuzzy feelings we get from reading about these legitimate heroes, especially if the article never challenges us to do the same.

We have a healthy dose of hero worship in this country. We might even have an addiction. We spend millions at our local movie houses and video stores to watch fictitious heroes run, jump, kick, shoot, lie and curse their way to victory. With popcorn on our breath we indulge ourselves in unrealistic adventures; and the more fantastic, the better. The idea of one person with a few sidekicks making such a huge difference on his terms in our society turns us on. It seems to make us walk taller and step livelier without initiating any real change in our own lives.

Like Jonah, many of us who enjoy more comfortable lifestyles are comfortably napping in response to those in harsh living environments. The day-to-day struggles that the less fortunate must endure hardly raise an eyebrow on many who have been blessed by the Lord. We're flat-out asleep when it comes to what is being done to others in our nation, many of whom are related to us by the blood of Jesus Christ.

William Scarlett writes in his exposition on Jonah,

"Jonah was as fast asleep as we Christian people have been, professing maximum Christian ideals but being content with a minimum of social action to achieve them. Two thousand years of preaching the brotherhood of man, and our world trapped in a barbed-wire entanglement. Two thousand years of preaching dignity and sacredness of every individual, and racialism still lifting its ugly head. And since the ideals we profess no longer protect these people, it is not to be wondered at if they rebel even against the ideals themselves." *(The Interpreter's Bible,* v.6, p.882; Abingdon Press, 1956.)

These words were written over 40 years ago, yet they still ring true. We have been good at preaching the message of hope and dignity to the masses in this country. We've preached it, sang it, written it, danced to it, shouted it, clapped it, cried over it, received degrees for it, laid hands on it and even rededicated our lives to the pursuit of it. But for the most part, we haven't *lived* the Christian life that is part of our heritage: the life dedicated to God that stands for justice and equality.

Selective Ignorance, Selective Justice
Since the so-called "trial of the century" has come and gone, an uproar has sounded across the land. It's the sound of millions of normally quiet citizens (many of whom are Christian) calling for justice. Months after the long-awaited verdict was announced, television and radio talk shows are still full of opinionated audiences weighing in on the subject. Eyes often fill with water and voices choke with emotion at the very idea that a man could be freed with so much evidence against him. Tabloids and editorials still scream for justice for the victims and their families. Friendships have been torn apart by the verdict. The issue of justice is squarely facing our nation, and at times it seems that America is finally getting a desire to do the right thing. Or are we?
At first glance, it would appear that we've received our wake-up call. After all, the amount of noise being made over one trial would tend to show that we have decided to become advocates for those people who are victims in this country. That means, of course, that we are now going to see a loud

voice raised on behalf of those who are not given equal
access to good housing or the loans to buy them. It appears
as though we will have demonstrations in the streets to find
out who really is behind the dumping of illegal drugs into
select communities. Protesters will ask, "How can we track
satellites out in deep space and can't track the trail of drugs
from our borders into these poor neighborhoods?" In fact, I
imagine you'll be hearing any day now about the marches
against injustice all over our land. Those who have been
voiceless for so long will now be heard by, and held by,
those who have been privileged to at least have met Mr.
Justice, right?

You know better. Because of the astounding amount of
rage over one murder case, we think things are changing. But
a further review of the facts brings a reality check: what we
have here is more of the same old "selective justice" thing.
The reality is that our country and way too much of the
church have no real desire or interest in justice for everyone.

We take on the spirit of Jonah when we pick and choose
for whom we will cry out. Jonah had the anointing and
power of God in his life, and with that anointing and power
also came responsibility. He was responsible to God, who
called him to fulfill his role as God's representative in the
earth. We, too, have a responsibility to God to show the
world Christ's love and compassion on the people of the
earth. But it is painfully apparent that we pick and choose the
causes as well as the people for whom we will activate our
Christian principles. We often show more zeal for snail
darters and whales than for our fellow man.

Isaiah 59:4 recounts one reason for God's anger against
his people:

No one calls for justice.

After all God had done for these people, they still
wouldn't stand up and be counted. After all the justice God
had wrought on their behalf, these people would not speak up

for the cause of justice when it was their turn. The same can be said about our generation. So many of us have been the recipients of justice, and yet we refuse to stand for it when others are in need of the same.

We must put justice into practice. There's an Iroquois saying, "Righteousness means justice practiced between men and between nations." Ignorance has been an effective excuse for not fulfilling our orders to love one another. "People just don't know what is going on in 'those communities' with 'those people'" is the excuse heard too often concerning problems in this country. No one can be on top of every issue, but we cannot deny that most of us in the American church have turned the disease of "selective ignorance" into a fine art.

We have more than enough experts in more than enough categories in our churches to exhaust our desire for knowledge on issues of justice. We take pride in our concern and knowledge of people groups in the mission field who will never see our shores. But what of the people who live in our communities, work across the desk from us, or attend the same church? Do we know even the simplest facts about them or their cultures?

The sad fact is *we don't want to know*, and it's at this point in the process that selective ignorance goes beyond a sad fact into the realm of a cancer among us. We've moved so far from God's desire for us that we intentionally choose to remain ignorant about the conditions that surround us. For all intents and purposes, we've chosen to sleep our way through the journey. Like Jonah we don't have a real fear of what will happen to us. Why should we? We *are* God's chosen vessels, aren't we? God has always blessed our paths and answered our prayers, so we assume we're safe in thinking, "I'll just find a comfortable place to rest and sleep through this part of my journey." It's a dangerous assumption.

Who's Steering This Ship?

Often when we decide to disobey God, we force ourselves to align with those who don't know him. The same was true with Jonah. He found himself sharing a voyage with men who had their own gods. While they were religious men, they had no real relationship to the only wise God. Jonah didn't check with God as to the background or beliefs of his shipmates. He didn't care what their testimonies were as long as they were headed in the direction he wanted to go.

Isn't it amazing that so many of the members of the Body of Christ have the same mindset as Jonah? We've gotten into the boat with all kinds of people. We don't care about how they pray or if they pray as long as they are going in the direction we think want to go. Many of the conservative personalities that so many of our churches and leaders have prescribed to don't have a testimony of church attendance, much less salvation -- *but that doesn't seem to matter as long as they say what we think is right.* The same can be said about so many liberal celebrities that have been dubbed "champions of justice."

Granted, these personalities -- liberal and conservative alike -- have some valuable agenda that highlight issues largely dismissed by our society. Still, this fact remains: *without some divine direction, they also are misguided.* So why is it that we, the Body of Christ, feel so comfortable climbing into the vessels guided by these folks and allow ourselves to become spiritually dormant? As long as they continue on the course that we intentionally have chosen the voice of God doesn't matter to us; we sleep and hope that we can reach our new destination as soon as possible.

We've already discussed a few of the obvious ingredients to our modern day storm. No doubt the world is attempting to lighten the load it brought with them just to stay afloat.

But I thank God that in the midst of our journey he has allowed a storm to arise, because it has given birth to an astounding trend: *even as the worldly system claims to have all the answers, it is now constantly looking to the church for answers.* Politicians and social workers alike continue to name the church as the one organization that could help most in the midst of the turmoil gripping our society, although the reality of tangibly including the church in problem-solving strategies is still a stretch for many "experts." Still, presidents, candidates, and even leaders of other religions are imploring the Church of Jesus Christ to live up to its high calling. Sadly, when these leaders seek us out, they often find us sleeping as the worst set of social, criminal, moral and political storms of our lifetime rage around us. Is it any wonder that, when the world tries to jar us back into some sense of awareness of contemporary thought, we blink and stammer like a patient awakening from a year-long coma?

The worst irony of being caught asleep in these times is who we say we are and who we represent. If any group should be sensitive to social justice, it should be the church. If any group should be alarmed by the amount of crime and hopelessness perpetuated upon our children, it should be the church. If any group is going to be riled at the decay of our cities and schools, the church should be first in line. But too often, prophets within us and critics outside us must ask, "How can you sleep?" In the midst of all that's going on in this country, we are unaware -- frequently by choice -- and there appears to be nothing that can awaken us from our slumber.

It's an amazing act of God's grace that the lips of many of our chosen captains carry the beginning of the answer for us today. "Get up and call your god! Maybe he will take notice of us, and we will not perish." It is amazing how even those who don't believe in God will request your prayer if their very survival is at risk. Let's get over the fact that, for many of us, the request for prayer has been initiated by some outside the walls of the church. So be it: the call to arise from our slumber and call on the name of the Lord is indeed the first step in returning to the call of God in our lives. If we are ever to come to grips with where we are in history, the genesis of our voyage into obedience must start with prayer.

Genuine prayer, of course, includes the acknowledgment of sin. This may be the hardest thing for us to do in this nation. The admission of guilt, even guilt before God, is not part of the American way. But if we want to start fresh with God, we must start there. Next we must repent of our sin. It's not enough to be sorry; we must commit to never return to the thoughts and ways of our past. That course of inner action and outer demonstration allows us to truly look out on the world with fresh hearts and clear minds that are truly accessible to God.

Acknowledging reality and acting on our need to change before God will keep us honest -- and awake.

Chapter Five
What Have You Done?

Then the sailors said to each other, "Come, let us cast lots to find out who is responsible for this calamity." They cast lots and the lot fell on Jonah. This terrified them and they asked, "What have you done?" (They knew he was running away from the Lord, because he had already told them so.) (Jonah 1: 7, 10)

Jonah's shipmates fleshed out the old adage, "Self-preservation is the first law of nature."

These wily experts of the deep had lightened the ship's load to improve their chances of survival. That action proved futile, so the sailors called a prayer meeting to stir their own gods into action. But the gods to whom they called had no power in this matter. With the storm still raging about them, the sailors had another thought: perhaps if they cast lots, they could determine who was responsible for this storm.

As in other ancient lands, lots were used in Israel as a tool to make decisions. The word "lot" literally means "a pebble," but it was often just a thin piece of wood. Among the Jews, lots were used with the expectation that God would control how the lots fell, and thus give the right direction. Sometimes they were used to discover the culprit behind a crime, as in the case of Achan in Joshua 7:14. Lots were also to choose a king or others for office. Acts 1: 26 tells how a new apostle was chosen:

> *Then they cast lots, and the lot fell to Matthias, so he was added to the eleven apostles.*

When the question arose concerning the dividing of property, lots were often used to determine the outcome as prescribed in Numbers 26:55:

Be sure the land is distributed by lot.

In every biblical example above the supposition was that divine influence -- not blind chance or simple fate -- would ordain the way the lots fell. The decision indicated by the casting of lots was believed to be God's own.

The storm-drenched sailors knew that this was no ordinary storm they were facing. The winds were too fierce and the waves too high to be a run-of-the-mill tempest. These raging winds had to be the result of some horrific sin; someone had angered a heavenly power and was hiding on their ship. If they could pinpoint the origin of the offense, perhaps they could identify some form of sacrifice to appease this god of the storm. Since there were no volunteers that stepped forward to admit guilt or take the blame, they agreed among themselves to cast lots. Surely the appropriate god would tell them who was to blame for this tragedy in the making.

All the passengers were assembled together and the lots were cast among a nervous crew. Could it be one of them had done something unknowingly that had made a god angry? Maybe one of their old friends had a big secret with his private deity. The time had come to find out the truth, and when the lots came to rest the verdict was unanimous: Jonah was the one.

Immediately the sailors pummeled him with questions. "Tell us, who is responsible for making all this trouble for us? What do you do? Where do you come from? What is your country? From what people are you?" These men who were terrified for their own lives were now very interested in the life of this passenger who had come along for the journey. Jonah was not known among them. It's doubtful he shared the same roots as the sailors, but there was now an intimate connection with them: Jonah was responsible for their sure destruction. They were more than curious about his actions and background.

No-Comfort Credentials

Jonah was quick to testify concerning his faith. Without hesitation, Jonah began to give his credentials: "I am a Hebrew and I worship the Lord, the God of heaven, who made the sea and the land." Let's take a closer look at Jonah's testimony.

He states for the record, "I am a Hebrew." Israelites would often describe themselves as Hebrews when introducing themselves to foreigners. In Exodus 3:18 God says to Moses,

"The elders of Israel will listen to you. Then you and the elders are to go to the king of Egypt and say to him, 'The Lord, the God of the Hebrews, has met with us.'"

The basis of a Hebrew's introduction was a clear relationship with God.

Little wonder, then, that "I worship the Lord" is the next portion of Jonah's self-introduction. The phrase, however, is better translated "I fear the Lord." Jonah's confession highlights the contradiction between his confessed faith and his disobedient actions. The "fear of the Lord" signifies absolute trust in, and unwavering obedience to, God Almighty. Jonah proves how much of a hypocrite he is by using this term in the midst of disobeying God's command for his life.

The fear of the Lord leads to all kinds of blessings, including faith and the beginning of wisdom. Curiously, Jonah must have believed that he could ignore God's clear command and still count himself among the faithful.

Jonah also showed a glint of pride in the superiority of his God to the gods of the heathen sailors as he referred to "...the God of heaven, who made the sea and the land." The sailors knew at that moment that the Lord was no regional deity, but the Being who created the sea and earth on which they traveled. These sailors may have never heard of Jonah's chosen deity before, but it alarmed them to think they might be on the receiving end such a powerful God's anger.

The fact that Jonah was listing his credentials while calmly owning his disobedience in the face of destruction was no comfort to the sailors.

Love or Smugness: Choose One

Our generation has taken a journey into dangerous water as well. Like Jonah, we are traveling with others who have very little in common with us. We are indeed part of a larger community, but we have somehow allowed that community to define us, despite the fact that the only apparent kinship we have is that they're headed in a direction we want to go. Sometimes these "defining communities" are political, sometimes not. Still, we've often aligned ourselves with those who have no clue to -- or passion for -- the will of God. Jonah was guilty of what he did *not* do. Some church fathers would call that a "sin of omission." That's what we have in common with the disobedient prophet. We can't deny it. Just take a close look at what we *haven't* done effectively as the church of Jesus Christ in this nation.

For example, we haven't effectively shown the example of Christ in loving one another. Before you close this book for good, think a moment about the effort of local churches to reach out to the hurting people around them. Isn't it strange that many of our churches spend so much money and time on auxiliaries and programs that have no value to those who are suffering around us?

The level of genuine love and concern for the poor and disadvantaged is not nearly the same as it was only thirty years ago. We've spent thousands of hours and millions of dollars trying to impress God with our "edifice complexes" while he is interested seeing our faith in action on behalf of those who need it. We've bought into the popular "it's their fault" mentality in regard to the poor. If we can just blame the poor for being poor, and the hurt for staying in pain, we enjoy a sense of smug justification.

Could it be that the love and concern the church showed over the decades kept the storm from our doors? Could it be those outdated, old fashioned hours of devotion and care for the young in our communities actually kept crime and moral decay from those too young to understand what could befall them if they were not careful? In many a Christian circle, we've decided *not* to do those things that were profitable acts of service for our communities as well as ourselves. We've abandoned our nurturing role to "the experts" who are turning to us along with the needy and asking us to own our responsibilities. (When did the church and the federal government switch roles, anyway?)

Maybe one of the most glaring weaknesses in our past actions is the lack of genuine love among the races. I can say for a fact that I know some wonderful people in every ethnic group I've encountered. They are a proven part of my joy in being a member of the Body of Christ. I'm sure there are many who are reading this book who can say the same. But history cannot be denied, much less our present reality: we're a long way from where we should be in terms of racial harmony in the church.

I suppose it could be asked, "Why aren't you including all Americans in your challenge for racial harmony?" Here's why: God did not command that the world love one another, he said that to the church. As a matter of fact, Jesus said that the world would know us by our love for each other. The problem is that, far too often, those with little or no connection with the church have outdone us in pursuing racial harmony.

I believe our country would be in much better shape if we, the church of Jesus Christ, had heeded his call for us to love each other unconditionally years ago. Our nation's history reminds us that to do so would have made us stick out like proverbial sore thumbs.

Maybe we needed to. We are descendants of people who put laws in place that made it almost impossible for us to love each other across racial lines. The Jim Crow laws combined with the laws that governed Native Americans kept many of God's people separate. While we had some examples of Christians of different races loving and living together as equals in the past, those were indeed isolated occurrences. Most white churches simply didn't welcome members of other races into their membership, much less allowing them to exercise leadership. When blacks or other ethnic groups attended some of the so-called "open minded" white churches, they were often only allowed to sit in the balcony. For them, even going to the altar for prayer was often a forbidden act. This type of treatment forced them to start their own churches and Christian organizations where they could apply their God-given anointing and callings freely. This institutional separation was perfectly welcomed by the majority church, and was common place in this country except for a few exceptions.

Still, each segment of this divided body grew and showed excellent examples of God's hand on human flesh. In communities across the land the church made strides to better the corners where they were. Unfortunately, the division between races in the church has effectively kept the full anointing and glory of God from manifesting itself among this nation's cities, reservations and rural communities. Because we are a Body, we can never be as effective as we could be as long as we are divided. After all, God never sends half a prophet to do a whole prophet's job. In his sovereignty, God allowed the original church to spread out across the world. But we have never been told to divide ourselves because of hatred or intolerance.

The Non-History of Reconciliation

If the sands of time were to run out on us today, the history books would say much about the great Christian church of America. Volumes would be written about our accomplishments in the area of education. We would probably have chapters that dealt with the contributions of the church in the area of music. No doubt countless words would describe our heroes and their great deeds. But there is no doubt that any stain marking those pages would include one glaring fact: that we, the Body of Christ in the United States, did little to show love to each other across racial lines. Sunday mornings are still the most segregated hours in our country.

At some future point, some may begin to defend our history and say, "We tried to love each other. As a matter of fact, we had 'reconciliation movements' in the 1990's." We could show some fruitful times that grew out of these movements, but the reality to date is that very little has been reconciled, at least from the "colored" point of view. The truth be told, many people of color don't see much change in the climate of things once the conferences or meetings are done. Why? Fact in point: the very word "reconciliation" means to renew a friendship of relationship. How can you renew something you never had? This word "reconciliation" has been passed around like an offering plate – and it remains mostly empty.

The result of this lack of love? Suddenly the tide of society has turned from a friendly nod toward the church to suspicion of our motives and our faith. Those who were once friends of the church are now asking, "Whose fault is the storm we are going through?" Much of the hatred and lack of trust in our nation is being blamed on the church.

Whose Fault is the Storm?

Like any republic, we face trials that cause us to look inward. This country has had its share of crises and has come through most of them with flying colors. But in the 1990's, we seem to have sailed into the teeth of a storm we've never seen before.

One need only take a look at the daily newspaper to see what is happening all around us. Crime is marked by a new degree of violence and senselessness. For the first time in the history of the United States, our children are the poorest group of people in our country. Sexually transmitted diseases are not only at an epidemic rate, but are also taking on new forms that make them more likely to be lifelong companions than sexual partners. Financially, we stand at the brink of disaster with the national debt flying farther out of orbit every second. We've entered wars and conflicts without good reasons and found ourselves on the short end of victory against many we desired to take out of power. Many of those conflicts would have been won easily only a generation ago. Our leaders make promises that they quickly break once they enter office, leaving voters shaking their heads in the polling booth. Trust is at an all time low; fear is at all time high.

With the entire nation looking for answers, the church sits back without intention of taking any of the blame. Instead, we're asking the questions: How could a nation with so much dignity and pride become the leader in teen pregnancy? How could the country that was known for the "All-American Family" produce almost as many divorces as it has weddings? Many of us wonder what has happened to the innocence of youth that we knew. Why do we find ourselves running from our own children? What changed? Whose fault is it?

If lots were cast today, I'm convinced that many of them would fall on the church. Many of those with whom we've partnered are convinced it's partly our fault. Many who once

united with the church -- in business as well as pleasure --
are now pointing an accusing finger at us. They blame our
God for allowing such pain and suffering around them. They
blame us for not doing more to develop our youth, families
and communities. We are asked to pray for those who are the
victims of their own sin and disobedience, yet when we stand
up for our basic Christian beliefs we are called "hate
mongers" and "small-minded."

Make no mistake, *we must admit to our own sin.* We've
been very good at running from the will of God. When folks
ask us who we are and what we're about, we quickly return to
the "Jonah style of testimony," which includes talking about
how we reverence and worship the Lord. By doing so we
once again prove, like Jonah, our hypocrisy. While we speak
of true worship and adoration of the King of Kings, we also
demonstrate disobedience to him by our lack of fulfillment
of his most basic commands. We say we fear him, and we
refuse to get together across racial lines and love one
another. It doesn't stop there. We also refuse to work
together, live together or appreciate other cultures, yet we
say we worship and love God.

We have to face this truth: *there is no selective love when
it comes to God.* Consider what the Holy Spirit gave to John
the apostle:

*If anyone says, "I love God," yet hates his brother,
he is a liar. For anyone who does not love his brother,
whom he has seen, cannot love God , whom he has not
seen." (1 John 4:20)*

We either love each other or we don't. We either obey God's
commandments or we don't. And if we are not obedient, we
are in defiance of his will for us just as Jonah was.

Scripture indicates that after Jonah finished his speech,
the sailors became terrified. They went from a series of
exploratory questions right to the point: "*What have you
done?*" The second major question in this episode was quite

direct and emotionally charged; it was nothing less than an indictment from the sailors. They already knew what Jonah had done because he'd told them. *Why* he told them is left to sheer speculation. Maybe Jonah was just arrogant; maybe he may have wanted them to know the whole truth before they perished.

Whatever the case, the sailors could not believe that a man who claimed to know God so well could do something so stupid. Why would he make such a powerful God so angry? Had he no fear for his own life? And if his life was of no concern to him, *what about theirs?*

I've spoken to those who ask the same question of the American church today. If you know God is so powerful, how could you directly defy his command to you? How can you Christians claim to know his awesomeness and still openly disobey him? What are you doing? And if your life is of no concern to you, *what about ours?*

We give many answers to our deeds. We do studies and teach classes on our disobedience. Why we do it is strictly up to interpretation. Maybe we are just arrogant. Maybe we want the world to know the whole story and ask them to choose sides among our many divided groups.

As the sailors of Jonah's journey questioned and marveled at his cold and calculated actions, so our modern world wonders at our continued disobedience. The same world that accuses us rightly questions if we will ever live up to the call we've accepted. So many times we have heard from those we seek to win, "There are just too many hypocrites in the church." So many people who would "join our band" are convinced that things are far worse on the inside of our buildings than on the outside.

Many times, they're right. But isn't it funny that sometimes those who don't know God have a far more vivid picture of what's going on than we do? All too often someone will observe our disobedient or sinful behavior and

remark, "I thought you were a Christian." They're really
asking, "What have you done? How can you, of all people,
disobey the word of your God? You claim to know him
better than anyone, yet you choose to ignore him on issues
that even an outsider like me can understand. How can you
disobey?"

Good questions. What's our answer?

Chapter Six
Credibility Lost

"Pick me up and throw me into the sea," he replied, "and it will become calm. I know that it is my fault that this great storm has come upon you." Instead, the men did their best to row back to land. (Jonah 1:12-13)

As a prophet of God, Jonah had spent many of his days following the leading of the Lord. Because of the public relationship he had with God, many people no doubt trusted him. He had built a reputation of being someone in whom people could believe. Because credibility hangs on other people's trust and belief, it is likely that Jonah enjoyed great credibility with his Hebrew constituents.

Credibility is an honor in times of dishonor. Yet Jonah would jeopardize his credibility because of his dislike for the people who lived in the city of Nineveh. In fact, he would risk his relationship with the Creator of the universe because of this hatred.

Confession: A great beginning, but...

Jonah had come clean concerning his reasons for being on the boat. He had confessed to his disobedience to God. He had even informed the sailors of the God who was causing the storm. But that confession alone had no bearing on the intensity of the storm. The scriptures indicate in verse 11 that the sea was getting rougher and rougher. Curiously, as Jonah finishes his confession the God of heaven commands the wind and the waves to *increase* their fury. It was if God wanted Jonah to know that he was even more convinced that Jonah's disobedience should not go unpunished.

Jonah was aware of his sin. Yet flying in the face of God's command, he was somehow convinced that he was doing what was right. His confession -- or his self-deception, for that matter -- did not sway God's intent for the disobedient prophet.

The sailors had to be overwhelmed at the entire event. Their whole day had been turned upside down. But at least they knew what was really going on. Since Jonah was the one who had started this whole adventure, surely he'd know how to end it. So they turned to Jonah and asked him for advice.

There's an old saying, "If you want to know how to solve a problem go right to the source." In this case Jonah was the source of the problem. The sailors' question to Jonah was direct and to the point: "What should we do to you to make the sea calm down for us?" Notice the question was directed to Jonah and the end result had to do with their own welfare. They wanted the sea to calm down for them, not Jonah. Still, in order for that to happen they knew Jonah had to make some kind of amends.

These men were not familiar with Jonah's God, nor his ways. They were followers of many gods who desired particular sacrifices. So they had to ask Jonah questions like, "What sort of thing does your God desire in order to calm his temper? What does this God of yours really want? What kind of sacrifice does this God desire?" Only those who followed God as Jonah did could answer these questions correctly.

We find ourselves as the church in American in a time of confession. Across our land we find congregations, individuals and whole denominations confessing their past sins. These are not novices nor new converts for the most part, but the core of the Body of Christ. We have seen thousands of men in stadiums, pastors in pulpits, and heads of large church groups stand openly and confess long-standing wrongs.

The astounding confession of guilt by the church has left many an observer speechless. The tears and rejoicing alike have been fodder for the media. They *should* pay attention, for such confession could signal the beginning of revival nationwide. However, the revival is still not taking in much of the country. Apparently our confession of wrong in the midst of the storm, like Jonah's, is not enough.

Truth in Action?

We, as a people, must remember the command of God on our lives. His direction to us as has been quite clear. Yet our actions suggest that a simple confession of disobedience will cause the current national crisis to subside. The problem is this: *as it was in Jonah's day, so it is in ours. The mere confession of disobedience is not enough.* Even with our ceremonial confessions and foot washing services, the storm is getting rougher and rougher. What is our next move?

Jonah was sure he had the answer for the storm: "Pick me up and throw me into the sea," he replied, "and it will become calm. I know it is my fault that this great storm has come upon you." Jonah knew that his disobedience called for one remedy: a sacrifice. Jonah was ready to be the sacrifice that would save the lives of these men. God would not allow him to leave that territory alive, and he felt that the men in the boat should not perish with him.

At face value, Jonah's offer sounds noble. He was indeed willing to die so the men on the boat would live. They were not his countrymen, nor were they believers in his God, yet Jonah stood ready to give his life for them.

As noble as it sounds, that very fact begs the question, "So why wasn't Jonah willing to give his life to obey God and go to the people of Nineveh?" The answer is painfully simple: at closer examination we see Jonah's primary concern was not to obey God. He probably didn't care that much for the kind of men these sailors were at first, but once he spent time with them in a crisis and realized they were no different than himself, who knows? The sailors may have talked about their families and the homes they would leave behind if the ship sank. Perhaps Jonah even recognized himself in their fear and folly. Sadly, it's clear that without this calamity they would have remained nameless members of some other race to Jonah -- some of "those people" who simply weren't as good as he and his kind.

Jonah's suggestion seems very "Christian," doesn't it? "Pick me up and throw me into the sea. I know that it is my fault that this storm has come upon you. I will be the sacrifice that God desires." Yes, it is a confession of guilt. What marks Jonah's suggestion is what it doesn't offer: any willingness to return to Nineveh and do what God had asked of him. Any mention of a desire to return to the city and be the voice of God just isn't there.

Owning the Call

Should it be a surprise to the church in the United States of America that the storm has not subsided in our land? Why would God change his ways because of our 'sacrifice' when he did not change in the days of Jonah?

Like Jonah, we have confessed our sin in many cases. But those cases are still limited. Many of our churches, denominations, conferences (and many of us) continue to hang on to our profession of innocence like a child clings to her teddy bear. Make no mistake: those of us who have run people away from the cross with our arrogance, ignorance and pride will someday confess to our part of this tragedy. We can pray that, out of God's mercy, the confession will come this side of eternity.

The glaring omission that became so clear when Jonah made his confession is also obvious to God and the world as they await our confession of guilt: we must make and deliver on the promise to complete the task to which we were first called. Like Jonah, we are likely to admit when we are wrong when we are caught and exposed by the Holy Spirit. Because of our relationship with the Lord, we also know that God requires us as living sacrifices to quell the immediate storm. As hard as that may sound to the outsider, it is still lacking the thing God desires to hear from our lips and hearts. *God wants us to return and accomplish the thing He called us to do in the first place.*

As we look upon the landscape we call the church and search for those who are working in the vineyard, we notice there are very few who will cross the line of their hearts and work with (or even on behalf of) those they hate. It's still easier for the majority of the church in this country to work with, or for, those who look just like them. Choosing to work or to develop a friendship with someone of another race can be more easily accomplished in lands other than this one.

As much as anything, the area of evangelism points this out in the church. we have become "experts" in foreign missions and have no clue how the needy within our own shores survive. Please understand that I fully believe God has directed us to help those in need outside our borders. We've done some great work in that area. Sadly, though, our reality is that we've done a decent job in helping the uttermost parts of the world and almost ignored Jerusalem. The disproportionate amount of work and investment in foreign work as compared to domestic missions is a tragedy. Worst of all, we know it but we won't do anything about it.

The plight of our youth in this country cuts to the heart of crises in the family and the church. We've gained all types of knowledge in technical and academic fields, but we seem to have forgotten how to raise our own children. From the cradle to the jail, we have systematically abandoned our youth to raise themselves. While data shows most people come to know Christ before their twentieth birthday, most churches are very inept at youth or child evangelism. An

informal survey I recently took showed that churches
commonly spend less than five percent of our budgets on the
young -- one of the most fruitful audiences with whom to
share the Gospel -- and focus the vast majority of our
resources on adult services and evangelistic efforts that often
yield little or no harvest.

The same type of foolishness can be observed concerning
a desire to only support or work with those of our own
denominations. We have made a mockery of God's love by
showing it to those only who are part of our system of
religion. It is true we all have our own style of worship and
preaching that appeals to us, but we're deifying and
politicizing our preferences as never before. The hierarchy
and control of many of our churches and denominations are
more complicated and messy than the federal government.
Someone much wiser than I said that God loved the world so
much that he didn't send a committee. Think about it.

Our gestures of confession in these and other follies
amount to only one step in the right direction. Even with that
one feeble step we still tell God, "I'm not going to the city.
They don't deserve your mercy or your grace." We make the
decision even when we confess and do nothing to complete
God's mission in our lives. We're actually saying, "I'd rather
perish than obey God." God's plan for Nineveh was to save
its people through the ministry of the prophet. God's plan for
our nation is to save its people through the ministry of the
Body of Christ. No other group or prophet can do the work
that God has chosen us to do. Those great social programs
and well-meaning followers of other gods cannot accomplish
the work of the Body of Christ.

Isn't it interesting that the sailors -- the experts on the sea
-- asked a "landlubber" like Jonah what it would take to
make the storm go away? They were concerned about the
immediate danger and how to stop it. The leaders and
communities of our day are asking the church a similar

question. At the risk of coming under tough scrutiny from
their peers, they ask us time and again to get involved in
making solutions for our communities. They have often
found it to be "politically incorrect" to be linked to
Christians. We bring all kinds of heat to the association, but
they keep asking. Still, what were intended to develop into
relationships of mutuality often hit such rough water that the
very survival of many of these teams is at stake.

Credibility Crisis

Jonah found out that along with his disobedience came
another unwanted benefit: the loss of credibility. One would
think the sailors would have taken Jonah at his word that
their best course of action was to throw him overboard. After
all, they'd asked his advice. But instead of taking heed to
Jonah, the sailors "did their best to row back to land." The
Hebrew uses a word meaning "to dig" (with oars, of course)
to describe the forceful struggle of the sailors. Why would
these sailors ignore Jonah?

Let's look at the possible motives behind their action.
First, we have to consider that these heathen men who
worshipped other gods might have been more moral than the
man of God. They could have figured that the murder of this
man was too cruel a fate. Even though Jonah was willing to
see thousands perish, they were willing to risk their lives to
save his. That's not hard to imagine; the times we live in are
full of examples of unbelievers who show more love and
compassion and love than the Church. Even (maybe
especially) when it comes to accepting a backslider or one
who has lost his way, unbelievers often show more "Jesus"
than the Christians do.

Second, the sailors might have believed that if they killed
the prophet of the God who was powerful enough to cause
the storm around them, that same God would certainly
destroy them. Perhaps, then, they thought it would be to their

advantage to get Jonah back to shore so they could receive some fabulous blessing or, at the very least, God's mercy.

The crew might have surmised that Jonah was so distraught that he was suicidal, and God would hold them responsible for the prophet's death even if he perished at his own request. This could account for their "digging" the oars into an already fierce set of waves.

The most reasonable conclusion, however, seems to be this: the sailors simply did not believe Jonah. He had already been guilty of disobeying his own God. He showed no respect for his God by sleeping during a time when he should at least been offering a sacrifice. Jonah further complicates matters by hiding his guilt at first, only being discovered through the casting of lots. Then, when confronted with his disobedience, he admits his wrongdoing -- *but even these "pagans" could tell Jonah's admission was not seasoned with the least bit of repentance.*

Why should these men, who were engaged in a battle for their very lives, have believed this liar Jonah? Jonah could have avoided this whole mess by doing the right thing in the beginning. Instead he leaned on his relationship with God like a crutch, without any concern for those on the boat or in Nineveh. They had no faith in him or his request. He was still a prophet, but he had lost his credibility.

Have you ever wondered why people ask for help and then ignore it? Why would people say, "Pray for us," and never attend one church service with us? Why are we asked to give our advice at numerous meetings just to have it thrown to the side like last Sunday's newspaper when it's time to take action? In some cases, I'm sure the answer can be attributed to the sinful nature of our society. But let's not kid ourselves: in many more instances, the reason we're ignored has to do with our track record. Like it or not, many of our worst experiences with unbelievers are our fault.

We are to be a light on a hill. We are watched more critically than any group in our neighborhood or nation. Our history has been documented not only by Christian historians, but also by those who have no belief in God.

That means many of our mistakes are part of the public record. We have played the starring roles in countless numbers of scandals and misguided deeds. And before we get defensive about our faults, we must remember that we are the ones who claim to have the answers to the problems of life. Just "trust and obey," right? Yet we have made a mockery of our own faith by running from the very things God has asked us to do.

We've been found sleeping when we should have been hard at work, and our slumber should not be mistaken for resting in the Lord. While the world has been busy taking over the very minds of our children, our churches are closed up tight virtually every hour of the week. So when does the general public have access to us outside of our celebration services on Sunday?

Too often the public has witnessed our fighting among ourselves. Why is it that many of our best attempts at warfare have been against each other instead of against the powers and principalities? Our church buildings are the scenes of many ungodly battles that have absolutely nothing to do with God or his calling on us.

We've yet to mention our fight to keep as isolated as we can from those who are different, and we must count this never-ending battle at the heart of the distrust the country holds for us.

Even with this undeniable, unflattering history, we have the audacity to believe people will believe us when we say, "Here is the way, walk in it." The world has a hard time believing we love them when we continue to show we have a hard time loving each other.

Tell me: if you were outside the church, would *you* trust us?

The Agenda of the Spirit

Even the fierce efforts of such skilled sailors to get Jonah back to the shore were to no avail. The Scripture simply says "the sea grew even wilder than before." God's plan for Jonah called for more than a return boat ride to the land.

As he watched the sea churn ever more violently around him, Jonah probably thought he was facing certain death. As he saw these seaworthy men fail against the strength of the storm that God sent, Jonah's thoughts may have flashed back to the time when the strength of the Almighty was in his favor. But on this day, the very hand that guided the prophet's footsteps was laying waste to any alternate plans he might have had.

We can see the same plight for our generation. The experts we have hired, befriended or volunteered to partner with have made plans to get us back to where we should have been all along. In many cases they, too, refuse to completely dump us off the boat. Hear this, though: things are not the same as they were in times past, for the wind of the Spirit is blowing across our land. He seems to have a particular agenda directed straight at us. No matter what the answers or antidotes of the well-meaning, God still appears to have another agenda for his people.

After all, *we* put ourselves the midst of this storm. Don't count on the men and women who have degrees and diplomas to make the storm cease. This time it will take more than the experts of our generation to save us from the clutches of disaster. The church knows today just as Jonah knew that this storm is our fault.

In Jonah's day, God would have not sent a storm to ravage the unbelieving crew if Jonah had not been on their ship. We sit in our pews and make judgments against the world and blame them for all the sorrow in our land. Each day we see more storms on the horizon and point a sanctified finger at the general public. But sinners have been sinning since Adam and Eve. It is their nature to sin; that's why they are called sinners. Unfortunately, we believe only sinners can anger God. The truth is, so can sinners saved by grace -- and we have much more for which to be accountable.

We, like Jonah, must come to grips with the place we have put ourselves. The credibility we once had with men is seriously shaken today. What's worse, our credibility with God is also in jeopardy.

Chapter Seven
A Vessel of Opportunity

But the Lord provided a great fish to swallow Jonah...
(Jonah 1:17)

What do you do when your options are exhausted?

The sailors had run out of options when it came to Jonah. They had tried to row him back to land, but to no avail. The winds and the waves were too much for even their expert maneuvers. The only option was the one suggested by Jonah himself: they had to throw the disobedient prophet overboard.

Even as they prepared to take hold of Jonah, the sailors apologized to his God:

> *Then they cried to the Lord, "O Lord, please do not hold us accountable for killing an innocent man, for you, O Lord, have done as you pleased." (Jonah 1:14)*

Notice that the direction of their repentance is not toward Jonah, but toward God. They were no longer worried about Jonah's safety or his thoughts. The only concern at this point was the mercy of God concerning the safety of the crew. Jonah had his opportunity to have an impact upon the men, but that time had passed.

Curiously, the sailors described Jonah as an "innocent man." It is commonly believed to be a term they used for God's sake, not for Jonah's. The sailors understood that this man had caused God's anger in the first place, but by using the phrase in reference to Jonah, they were covering themselves from blame should it be discovered that Jonah really was innocent to a degree that deserved something other than a death sentence.

The next step was self-evident and swift:

*Then they took Jonah and threw him overboard, and
the raging sea grew calm. (Jonah 1:15)*

Jonah did not jump, and it doesn't appear that the sailors
gave him that opportunity, either. He was taken forcibly and
thrown off like a mutineer. Facing certain death, it's curious
that Jonah did not fight or scream for his life. To his credit he
gave no excuses, nor did he offer any new solutions. It was
the time of reckoning and Jonah faced it without a fight.

As soon as Jonah was dispatched into the waters' depths,
the storm ceased. It was a miracle of nature in the eyes of the
sailors. The fierce supernatural storm that seemed to have a
life of its own simply vanished. It was clear that the purpose
of the storm was to stop Jonah from proceeding with his
plans. When the storm's mission was accomplished it was of
no more purpose to God, so he called off the wind and the
waves.

The lesson in this passage of scripture is quite clear.
When God allows a storm to enter our lives, often its purpose
is to get us to take another course. He allows storms to test,
prove, and turn our paths back to him. When we comply to
the wishes of God, many of life's storms will cease. He
doesn't take pleasure in our discomfort, only in our
obedience and faith. Many of the "storms" we experience are
simply being obedient to God, as we should be. God's storms
will only place us where God desires. If a trial is from God, it
will quickly cease when its mission is accomplished.

The sudden transformation of weather had a strange
effect upon the sailors:

*At this the men greatly feared the Lord, and they
offered a sacrifice to the Lord and made vows to him.
(Jonah 1:16)*

Don't make too much of this; there is no evidence that the
sailors gave up on their local deities. Ancient pagans, much
like their modern counterparts, were ready to recognize any
number of gods and the influence those gods might have on

the circumstances around them. In this case, the sailors on
Jonah's boat affirmed that the God of Jonah had made
himself known through the storm, and that they owed him
some honor for letting them survive.

As far as the sailors were concerned the story and life of
Jonah, the disobedient man of God, were over. No man could
survive the long journey back to shore. Even though the
fierce winds and waves of the storm were over, the water was
still too deep and cold for a mere human to survive for long.
So the sailors went on their way, and no one suggested that
they go back and get Jonah now that the storm was gone. In
their minds he was an unusual sacrifice to his God. This
adventure would make a good fireside story for their friends
and families to marvel at and discuss. The man they called
Jonah was sure to be remembered for his sorry end.

Setting Up for a Sorry End?

Our position today is undeniably like that of Jonah's on
his way overboard.

Many of the people who fought for our survival as a
church are now throwing up their hands and giving up. Some
who at least acknowledged our worth in society at one time
are now separating themselves from the Body of Christ.
They have unceremoniously sacrificed us for their own
survival, offering us platitudes and political compliments
while cutting the jugular of our identity -- and integrity -- as
the people of God.

At the same time God's words are used for speeches and
benedictions in statehouses and campaigns, the church and
her views are quickly pushed overboard. So often today God
is being invoked while his Bride is being trashed. It's not that
so many of those considered powerful today have given their
lives over to the lordship of Christ and aren't walking the
walk of a disciple. It's that so many of those men and women
who acknowledge the existence of our God are no different

than the sailors of Jonah's day. The reality is that they are ready to recognize the existence and power of many gods. As proof, one need only take a look at our leaders in the United States who put their stamp of approval on any deity or god that is "politically correct" for the moment.

It also appears that we have become a byword in the story of our own land. That's right: the once respected and revered church of America is now reduced to a role as a bit player in our country's theater. On the one hand, we are indeed being sought out for leadership in problem areas. On the other hand, are rarely asked to take a tangible role to impact the White House or public housing. We must share the stage with all forms of gods and devils in order to be heard at all. In the eyes of many we are no better than the witches and psychics that star on the daily infomercials.

Some look at our present condition as the end of our story. We are looked upon as a once great force, with its best days far behind it. Could it be that the Church of the United States is left to only count its former victories? Is God done with us?

God's Provision

Remember this: *the Lord provided a great fish to swallow Jonah.* Just when things seemed to be hopeless for Jonah, God stepped in to rescue him. The same God who caused the terrific storm that changed his plans sent help. "Help?" you might ask. "How could a monster of a fish be help to a drowning man?"

So often, we've studied and sung about Jonah and "the whale" in an amusing way. We've taught our children that the fish was a punishment for Jonah's disobedience. Nothing could be further from the truth. As we take a closer look at this passage we'll understand that this fish indeed was a vessel of opportunity.

Scripture indicates that the God of Jonah *provided* a great fish. The word "provided" means "to procure beforehand; to prepare; to supply; to stipulate previously." God had prepared this animal ahead of time for Jonah's benefit. He knew that Jonah would need this fish before Jonah knew it. Even though Jonah had been disobedient to God and had his own plans for the people of the city of Nineveh, God still loved him and had plans for him.

Some may think that the possibility of God having a fish ready to swallow Jonah makes God look too much like a cosmic mechanic. If God would orchestrate all of Jonah's moves, he is nothing more than a puppet master. However, it is clear that Jonah made his own decisions just as we do. God in his infinite wisdom and love intervened in Jonah's life, which is his right with all of us.

What about the great fish? What was its real purpose? Some writers argue it was just a fairy tale created for our benefit to make a point. They say no such animal ever existed and it is just an old story that was common in Jonah's day. It is true there were old folk tales in Greece, Rome, Persia, India and Palestine that mentioned large fish or whales that swallowed men whole. These stories have led many to come to the conclusion that Jonah's story was just another of those make-believe tales.

The role of the fish in the life and survival of Jonah is backed up by our Lord himself, who made reference to Jonah's story as historical fact when he illustrated his own death, burial and resurrection in Matthew 12:39-41. To me, it seems clear that Jesus was recounting Jonah's story with the same sense of historical purpose as his own death and resurrection. That places Jonah's experience as a miracle of God's intervention in real life.

It is clear that the fish was there at God's direction to be a provision for Jonah. He was, indeed, in need of help. No matter how good a swimmer he might have been, the distance from land would have prevented him from swimming to shore. The Lord had not allowed the sailors the ability needed to get him back to where he should have been all along. He was not provided a life raft, or even a life preserver.

If there had been any witnesses to the actual swallowing of Jonah they surely would have concluded that God sent the fish to kill the man. As the fish approached Jonah, I'm sure he thought it was there to kill him also. But things aren't always as they seem; instead of this animal being the monster it may have appeared to be, it became Jonah's vessel of opportunity.

Jonah's Custom-Built Prayer Closet

God provided this fish so that Jonah would have the opportunity to survive. "Survival" is defined as "living beyond the life of another person, thing or event." Jonah was being permitted a life beyond his disobedience, the storm and the water in which he found himself imprisoned. The fish that many of us previously looked upon as a punishment was in reality a vessel of opportunity for Jonah's deliverance. God in his wisdom prepared a self-contained, self-propelled combination prayer closet and submarine for Jonah.

For three days and three nights the inside of the fish was home for Jonah. Admittedly, this was probably not the most comfortable place in the world to be. The smell and sticky walls of the fish must have been horrible, but Jonah was still alive. He was alone and isolated, but he was still alive. He was no doubt hungry, but he was still alive. The world had forgotten about him and written him off, but he was still alive.

Because God had spared him, even in the belly of the fish Jonah's priorities were apparently restored:

> *From inside the fish Jonah prayed to the Lord his God. (Jonah 2:1)*

For the first time in this account of Jonah's story we notice
Jonah praying to his God. Until we reach chapter 2 of Jonah
all communication attempts are coming from God to Jonah.
Now in the belly of the great fish, Jonah cries out to the
Lord.

> *He said: "In my distress I called to the Lord, and he*
> *answered me." (Jonah 2:2a)*

Amazingly, the same man who had completely disobeyed his
God recalled his mercy at the moment of his own distress.
Jonah offered thanksgiving for deliverance from death in the
sea. Jonah recalled his prayer for help as he was sinking into
the depths. His gratitude was heightened by his knowledge
that he deserved death, but God had shown him
extraordinary mercy.

"Distress" is defined as "affliction; anguish of body or
mind; a state of danger; destitution." Affliction or distress is
often a blessing in disguise. Consider Psalm 119:67:

> *Before I was afflicted I went astray, but now I obey*
> *your word.*

As did the Psalmist, so Jonah came to his senses as
death crept over him. His testimony given in verses 2-7 once
again shows God's endless mercy to his people.

> *From the depths of the grave I called for help, and*
> *you listened to my cry. You hurled me into the deep, into*
> *the very heart of the seas and the currents swirled about*
> *me; all your waves and breakers swept over me. I said, I*
> *have been banished from your sight; yet I will look again*
> *toward your holy temple. The engulfing waters*
> *threatened me, the deep surrounded me; seaweed was*
> *wrapped around my head. To the roots of the mountains I*
> *sank down; the earth beneath barred me in forever. But*
> *you brought my life up from the pit, O Lord my God.*
> *When my life was ebbing away, I remembered you, Lord,*
> *and my prayer rose to you, to your holy temple.*

"From the depths of the grave" indicates that Jonah believed he had come close to death in this experience. His recognition that God used the sailors to throw him into the sea is made evident in his confession, "You hurled me into the sea," and the phrase "the very heart of the sea" is used in scripture to depict being completely out of sight.

What the above verses make plain is the clear hopelessness of the situation. Jonah realized that he was separated from his God -- *and that nothing else was important.* Then the vessel of opportunity is introduced to the prophet; the terrible monster that the world describes comes along and brings an opportunity for life "up from the pit." So, at what he thought was the very end of his life, Jonah remembered his heavenly Father. He recalled the goodness of God and understood again who God really was to him. Though he was far from the temple in Jerusalem, he cried out from his heart to his God's heavenly temple.

Then Jonah started to come to grips with his own idolatry:

> *Those who cling to worthless idols forfeit the grace*
> *that could be theirs. (Jonah 2:8)*

Jonah realized that much of what he clung to was worthless. His hate for the people of the city was worth nothing. And because he held fast to it, he forfeited the grace and mercy of God in his own life. He made a mistake of hanging onto a hatred that drug him down to the bottom of the sea, and nearly cost him his life.

Clinging to What Counts

If we are to see revival in our land we must come to grips with our situation. Our very existence as a viable tool of God in the land is in jeopardy. There is no doubt in my mind that if we don't do the work God has called us to do, he will raise a group of people that will obey him.

Let's hope it doesn't get to that point.

Many of us have realized that things aren't right between God and us. We look like the people of God. We walk like the people of God. We have the titles and the positions within our own congregations. However, God's glory is not with many of us.

In literature, and in Scripture, water often represents those things we can see, touch and experience -- but not control. Frequently in the Bible, it presents a barrier or obstacle. For Jonah, water was an all-consuming sea that made him appear as only a speck upon its surface. More threatening was its ability to swallow him whole and hide him from the world forever.

Today we are surrounded by a sea of seemingly uncontrollable forces. Hopelessness, poverty, drugs, violence, sexual sins and countless other destructive forces surround us. Somehow we've allowed the things that we once held captive to have the victory over us.

Jonah's hatred for Nineveh is much like our hatred for those who are different from us. Like Jonah, we've nurtured our hatred for one another until it, like other "anchors," has drug us down. Many of us are in tight places because we refuse to let go of our prejudice and hate. We're sinking as God calls us to accountability because there is no place for racism, classism or any other type of cliquish behavior in the Body of Christ.

What was true for Jonah is true for us today in the realm of repentance, too. In the depths of the uncontrollable sea, Jonah remembered God. Even though he was "the man of God," that reputation did him no good in his stressful situation. Yes, he probably had many great testimonies he could point back to, but that did him no good where he was. So Jonah thought of the One who made him who he was. Jonah recalled the One who had given him the peace that passed all understanding.

Our lives mirror Jonah's in many ways, and none more than his fall from grace. As we ponder our futures, and our future together, please give these words some thought. Your reputation may be great, but without God it is nothing. You may worship in the finest of churches, but without God it is nothing. Your bank account may be enviable, but without the blessing of God upon your life you might as well be bankrupt. It's this simple: unless we remember the God of our salvation we will perish. The things he has provided for us are not enough to save us from the sure destruction we will suffer if we don't obey him.

So many of us currently find ourselves in a place of isolation. We're lonely, even though there are people all around us. Some of us are extremely uncomfortable with our present lives. Many of us find ourselves in sticky situations that we'd soon forget. But we are still alive.

Because of our isolation or discomfort many of us find ourselves calling out to God. Be glad for the opportunity you now have to call out to God. Many of those who have gone on to eternity never found the peace you can, if you will. I'm not speaking of your salvation; that was paid for by Christ. Nothing you can do will stop the work of Christ on the cross. However, we as the Church in America must own this: for years, we have forfeited the full grace of God by clinging to the hatred and prejudice that God hates.

Neither should we deny that we are drowning. We need a vessel of opportunity, and that vessel is upon us. It is time to remember God. It is time to call out to him. It is time for us, as the representation of Christ on the earth, to stand together as one and realize the strength of God in us.

We have the opportunity to be the first generation in the history of our country to stand as the Body of Christ united. We have the opportunity to show the world the strength and the power of Christ's love in people of different colors, ages and backgrounds. We have the opportunity to show God we love him more than we love ourselves.

The opportunity is here for us to be heroes in a time when they are too few.

Chapter Eight
A Second Time

Then the word of the Lord came to Jonah a second time...(Jonah 3:1)

After all the negative things Jonah had said and done, our Lord still had a plan for his life.

From inside the fish's belly he remembered a psalm that struck close to home. That psalm was one of thanksgiving for deliverance from death; a death he deserved and expected. But God in his own way had shown Jonah unexpected mercy in his time of need.

As Jonah's psalm from the belly of the fish ends, the prophet makes the statement God wanted to hear from the very beginning:

But I, with a song of thanksgiving, will sacrifice to you. What I have vowed I will make good. Salvation comes from the Lord. (Jonah 2:9)

Scripture does not indicate how long Jonah occupied his living condominium before he came to this point of decision. We do know he was inside the fish three days and three nights all totaled. Seventy-two hours is a very long time to endure the strange sounds, smells and motions inside a living creature. Added to those unusual surroundings was complete darkness. Since he had no manner of building a fire and fish aren't created with windows, he spent the whole time in the dark.

For those who insist that this story is only a parable of the children of Israel in captivity, please reconsider. The idea of a man being swallowed whole by a fish is indeed a strange tale. However, there are accounts of a fisherman being swallowed by a sperm whale and later being found alive and intact. There's no question such a phenomenon is rare, but it can occur. Remember, as I mentioned earlier, Jesus recounted the story of Jonah's adventure when describing his own death, burial and resurrection. Not once did the Savior indicate that Jonah's adventure inside the fish was fiction. That's why we need to think comprehensively about Jonah's situation.

To begin, one would assume that his first few hours inside this fish were not exactly soothing. We could also assume that he still expected to die, and to die a slow, agonizing death. Jonah may have believed the great fish was God's chosen vessel through which to kill him, and that the only reason God had allowed the fish to swallow him whole was that God wanted him to think about his hate and disobedience before his death.

But Jonah's thoughts eventually moved backed to God's love and faithfulness. Eventually, even from the fish's belly, Jonah understood that the reason for his situation wasn't God's hatred of him. Rather, it was the Lord's desire to see the people in Nineveh saved. God would indeed require a sacrifice from Jonah: obedience to his original call.

The origin of men making sacrifices to God is itself a question for history. Whether it was from an external command, or whether it was based on that sense of sin and lost communion with God, cannot be traced. Jonah's particular sacrifice to God was not only steeped in his own sense of guilt and sin, but also in gratefulness. He was no stranger to the ways of the Father; Jonah was sure of what the Lord required. This desire to do God's will was indeed a sacrifice for Jonah. His heart had not changed toward the people of Nineveh, but he loved the Lord and understood that God's desire for him was that he preach salvation to those who were in that city.

Let me emphasize again that Jonah's deep love for God did not do away with his abiding hatred for "those people" living within Nineveh's walls. By changing his mind about going to the city, Jonah was sacrificing his own desires in exchange for the will of God. Jonah's desire was still to see the Ninevites perish in their sin. And why shouldn't "those people" perish? Nineveh had a long history of making life and death miserable events for Israel. The very thought of them repenting and finding grace and mercy after the history they amassed was more than Jonah could imagine. But the events of the previous days coupled with Jonah's dilemma inside the fish no doubt led him to realize God intended him to carry out his role as a prophet. Though Jonah disliked the people in Nineveh, his desire to leave the descendants of Nimrod without hope was not his to make. God had made the decision and Jonah had been chosen to carry out the task of proclaiming judgment on the people of the city.

In the Book of Psalms, prayers were commonly accompanied by vows. These vows usually accompanied thank offerings:

Sacrifice thank offerings to God, fulfill your vows to the Most High, and call upon me in the day of trouble; I will deliver you, and you will honor me. (Psalm 50:14)

I am under vows to you, O God; I will present my thank offerings to you. (Psalms 56:12)

A vow is a solemn promise made to God to perform or to abstain from performing a certain thing. Vows were entirely voluntary, but once made they were regarded as an obligation. There are no indications here that God asked Jonah to vow anything to him. There had been no mention of vows before this time. Perhaps Jonah was thinking about his implied vow of obedience as a prophet of God. Perhaps Jonah made a specific vow to God regarding Nineveh while he was in distress. Whatever the case, God's grace became sufficient again for the prophet to fulfill his vow to God.

The result? Jonah was willing to complete the task of a prophet, no matter what his personal feelings about the task. At the same time, Jonah's thoughts turned away from death to the conviction that God would allow him to complete his task. Again, it is important to note that Jonah had not changed the way he felt about the people of Nineveh. God had given him ample opportunity to ask for grace in understanding "those people," but Jonah didn't even ask God why he wanted to give Nineveh one last chance. He didn't want to know. Even after the terrible consequences he faced, Jonah still hated the people of Nineveh so much that his heart's desire to see them destroyed was still there. However, Jonah's love for God was greater than his hatred for Nineveh.

Stages of the Journey

Our journey as the Church of Jesus Christ in the United States finds us at different stages in a voyage like Jonah's. Some of us have disobeyed God and are knowingly headed in the wrong direction; God's will is simply contrary to the place we want to be. It could be because the road he wishes for us is not profitable enough. Maybe some of us are convinced that those to whom God would have us minister deserve the fate that awaits them without his mercy.

Others find themselves safe on "The Old Ship of Zion" sleeping the time away. Many of us consider the weekly sermon our complete experience with God. Some of us have been "found out." We've been uncovered as the cause of distress for our acquaintances, friends or family. Sad as it is, we can't deny that too many of the problems in our homes and communities can directly be tied to the disobedience of God's people. Until we admit the sin that *we* have committed, we can expect sin around us to continue to grow in our homes, churches, neighborhoods and cities.

There are some of us knee deep in fish guts and darkness wondering if we will survive. In Jonah's case, he was in his vessel of opportunity but had yet to recognize it at that point. The analogy means we've been rescued from our own disobedience and we don't know it.

How many of us will admit that we've volunteered ourselves for calamity from time to time, only to have the Lord prepare some divine way of escape for us? Those forms of escape aren't always to our liking. God's choice of transportation may not be the mode we would have chosen, but the direction it takes us is the way we should have been going all along. There are some of us who have lost our reputations and maybe even more just to find ourselves in God's will.

In 1995 I was among thousands at the Azusa Conference in Tulsa, Oklahoma as former television evangelist and president of the PTL Ministries, Jim Bakker, talk about his now-infamous ordeals. Among the many riveting remarks made by Bakker was one I'll never forget. He stated when commenting on his time in prison, "I lost everything I had. I lost my ministry. I lost my money. I even lost my wife.... But, I found Jesus."

Even with so much distrust and dislike among us, God has brought many of our number to a place where he can finally use us. This is the group that has come to the time of "sacrifice and vows." We, like Jonah, have our own flesh-taught, sin-based, stereotypical fears, hatreds and prejudices. While we have been bought with a price that we can't imagine in our wildest dreams, we still find it hard to discard some sins that so easily beset us. Many times God has asked us to overcome these sinful character flaws with love. He requests we be the example on the earth he spoke about in scripture. When we have met that challenge, revival and church growth has usually followed. Unfortunately, these examples of obedience are few.

Because of our disobedience, we have seasons of unrest in our own hearts. The "peace that passes understanding" has been disturbed. A startling number of individuals have told me that for them, the past several months have been filled with sleepless nights. They confess to having possessions that many would give years of their lives for, yet they still have trouble resting comfortably at night.

Recently a white man of great reputation shared his frustration with me. His troubles had nothing to do with the lack of money; he is paid very well by the ministry that employs him. There were no complications with his wife or children. God had blessed him with the privilege to travel whenever or wherever he likes. Still, his soul was troubled. God made it impossible for him to sleep with the knowledge he has concerning racial prejudice within the evangelical church.

His conversation with me started like a man making a confession. He recounted a meeting he attended with some other Christian leaders of the church and parachurch. "We were planning a reconciliation conference," he said. "But we planned the whole thing without any of your people (African Americans) there. When we invite your people to assist in the organization of these events, most of the decisions have already been made." He went on to tell me that this type of thing goes on all the time in the church. He is accustomed to hearing his colleagues jest about blacks. This behavior no longer sat well within his soul.

Blind at Midday

Isaiah 59:10 describes God's misguided people this way:

Like the blind we grope along the wall feeling our way like men without eyes. At midday we stumble as if it were twilight; among the strong we are like the weak.

Isaiah described a group of people who knew the love and mercy of God. At the same time they took advantage of his goodness by ignoring his commands to live holy lives. The center of their trouble was spiritual state of being: they were blind to the true things of God. They were so consumed with their own lusts, they could not see where they truly needed to be.

The second portion of this scripture speaks of a lost opportunity: "At midday we stumble as if it were twilight." While the sun is at its highest point and the path is easiest to see, the writer compares these people to those who are feeling their way through a dark house. Such a dramatic description could be used today to indicate our sense of futility.

We're actually living in one of the greatest times for evangelism. The opportunities to change lives for the kingdom of God are endless. The world is looking for a savior. However, we seem to be headed down this path of opportunity like the blind without a cane or a seeing eye dog. Ignoring the obvious, we've become as blind as those who need help. Nevertheless, many are coming to the realization that God has spared our lives and our ministries for such a time as this. The hour is upon us to present our bodies as a living sacrifice to God – *and the reasonable service that God requires from us calls for an honest assessment of our lives.* From the inside out, we must judge ourselves in the light of God's Word.

For some of us it didn't (or won't) take long to determine what God desires. Only a short time of isolation with our thoughts and God's Spirit and we are on our way to obedience. For others, however, the time it takes us to admit our shortcomings may take years. For others still that moment of truth will never come, at least not on this earth. But it will come.

For those who never escape the belly of the fish, your story has a very different ending than Jonah's. Unfortunately there are many who condoned the initial mentality of Jonah, even to the point of death. We still live among some who feel that cultural division is the will of God. In Christ's name, they preach a strange form of the Gospel that claims a separation defined by race is somehow desired by God. As the enlightened Church, we must deliberately identify our actions for what they are. Why? Because we deliberately disobeyed the Lord in the beginning of our journey. There are many mistakes that we have made as individuals and the body collect.

I cannot explain to you why this book has so much to say about racial prejudice in the church, but I'm as convinced that this is what God called me to write about as I am of my own name. We could spend an entire chapter discussing all the ways we've separated ourselves. In the American church, we've perfected the term "division." But now God is calling us to put aside our differences and go to the people together. Our work will not be complete until we learn to not only love one another, but also display that love publicly.

Some of what has happened in the church can be blamed on ignorance. That excuse has some merit; many good-hearted parishioners have been fixed in their pews Sunday after Sunday waiting for a fresh word from God. Unfortunately, pastors and evangelists have danced around the issues of love and acceptance quite skillfully. Because of lack of direction from the pulpit, something must be said for those who never fully understood God's call to love all people.

That being said, "ignorance" has a bad rap in the family of God. We pride ourselves concerning knowledge in this country. We say that we are the most intelligent nation in the world. Libraries are stocked with more information than we could possibly hope to explore. Yet we can't find the books and videos, much less the friendships, that would allow us to know each other.

Let's face it. Much of our ignorance is selective. We have chosen to be ignorant of those we don't like or care to know. While we must work with some of "those people" on our jobs, we don't have to worship with them so we *choose* not to worship with them. We may have to shop at the same stores with "those people," but that doesn't make us brothers. We choose not to ask questions that might destroy our stereotypes.

Deliverance on Dry Ground

At the end of Jonah 2, God speaks again. This time he speaks not to Jonah but to his aquatic vessel of deliverance:

And the Lord commanded the fish, and it vomited Jonah onto dry land. (Jonah 2:10)

When God speaks everything must obey. Whether the sea or the fish, when God's command is given the orders must be carried out. Only Jonah disobeyed during this story, and even he was turned by God.

At the command of God, the mighty fish swallowed God's reluctant child whole. At the command of God the fish released Jonah from his watery prison. We must be sure to understand that we, too, shall remain prisoners to whatever holds us until God speaks to it and commands it to let us go. When God commands whatever is holding us to let us go, it must let us go. Until that time nothing that God has told to hold us will release us.

Notice also Jonah was released upon *dry ground.* Scripture does not say what land it was, although it is presumed to be Palestine. Dry ground represents the place God always delivers his people. When the Children of Israel marched across the Red Sea floor it was on dry ground. When over forty years later the next generation of Israelites walked into the promise by way of the Jordan River, the Bible tells us that it was on dry ground.

"Dry ground" represents for us those places that have firm footing. The deliverance God provides is not messy or complicated. God has always done a thorough job when it comes to delivering his people. His desire for us is to leave the old place, and then come into his desired place for us ready and able to move. That isn't possible when the place where we find ourselves is "muddy."

So often we hear testimonies of what people call "God's deliverance." However, after close examination it is only a counterfeit. So many go from one bad situation to another and say God put them there. God's desire is for us to stand on dry, firm, steady, uncomplicated ground. Unless this describes your situation, don't say it was God who put you there. Yes, there are times when the Lord allows rough times in our lives. That's not the analogy I'm trying to make here; the point is, after our disobedience becomes obedience, God desires us to have a victorious testimony. God wants us to have a witness that displays us standing and walking in victory, not slipping and sliding with the rest of the world.

A Second Time

Then the word of the Lord came to Jonah a second time. (Jonah 3:1)

There was no one else there to witness Jonah's vow. There is no record of witnesses to his deliverance onto the dry ground. God, however, spoke to Jonah again.

"A second time" represented a second chance for Jonah. God gave Jonah a second chance to be the prophet he initially called him to be. There still is no evidence of repentance on Jonah's part for his sin against the Ninevites. He never acknowledges his sin of prejudice to God or anyone else. The single evidence that the severe circumstances Jonah had experienced had worked on him was the fact that he finally went to Nineveh.

Could this be the second time God is speaking to our generation concerning our own racism within the church? Could it be the second time for you? Only you can answer that question.

I truly believe that many who read this book will examine their hearts and repent of the sin of racial prejudice. No doubt other sins of hatred will be rebuked as well. Nevertheless, the sad truth is some of us will never repent. There are some sins so deeply imbedded in us we will never dig them out. They will accompany us all the days of our lives.

Even in that condition, some will go and fulfill God's command as did Jonah. But they will go without love, repentance or joy.

Chapter Nine
Jonah, You Still Have to Go to the City!

"Go to the great city of Nineveh and proclaim to it the message I give you." Jonah 3:2

Why does God choose us for missions in which we'd rather not take part? Why doesn't he choose us for the ones that make us feel good? Can't he see that there are some places and some people we would rather not be around, especially in his name? Doesn't he know that maybe some of "those people" aren't worth saving?

The same type of questions probably entered the heart and mind of Jonah. He had made it clear by his actions that the folks in Nineveh were the last group of people to whom he wanted to offer God's mercy. Jonah's preferences, of course, were of little consequence to God's call: God still wanted Jonah to proclaim his word to Nineveh.

Remember, the book of Jonah is *about* Jonah, too. God cared for him in a special way, just as he did for the folks in the city. God had a dual purpose for Jonah going to Nineveh. First, there was a need for his word to go forth in that great city. Second, there were some things in Jonah that could be healed in the process. God had a plan that could actually "kill two birds with one stone," or, as I put it growing up in the hood, "kill two roaches with one shoe." But God's plan could not be fulfilled for Jonah or Nineveh unless the prophet obeyed the command of God.

Scripture is quite clear on one thing: God doesn't change!

Repeating Instructions
The word of the Lord came to Jonah quite clearly at the beginning of this story:

*Go to the great city of Nineveh and preach against it,
because its wickedness has come up before me. (Jonah
1:2)*
These are the words the prophet heard that caused him to
cringe and run. The last thing that he wanted to do was go to
Nineveh. So, he ran away. From the speed of his decision
and the determination with which he ran, we can determine
he understood the implications of going to the city.
Jonah's determination made his decision almost fatal.
Having been through the tempest and the belly of the great
fish, Jonah had a new lease on life. God spoke to Jonah a
second time:
*Go to the great city of Nineveh and proclaim to it the
message I give you. (Jonah 3:2)*
Right away we notice that God had not changed his mind
about Jonah's destination. Jonah was to go to the city of
Nineveh. But, didn't God know that Jonah didn't want to be
there? Yes, he was very aware of Jonah's desire to never
place a foot in the city. The whole reason for the wind,
waves and the fish was to get Jonah to go to Nineveh.

There are some striking similarities between God's two
instances of instructing Jonah (verses 1:2 and 3:2). The most
obvious is the word "go." God gives a clear direction to
Jonah. He didn't tell him to write a letter to the people of
Nineveh; neither was there a call from God to pray for the
folks of Nineveh. We notice that God didn't tell him to raise
funds for missionaries to send to the city. There was no
urgent direction from God that Jonah should do a study of
the people groups of Nineveh and write a paper concerning
their activities. God didn't tell Jonah to build a monument or
a prayer tower. God didn't instruct Jonah to fast for three
days for Nineveh. While each of the preceding directives
could have made an impact on the people of the city, God
didn't see fit to direct Jonah to do any of these things. He
told Jonah to *go* to Nineveh.

God wanted to put Jonah in direct contact with the people of Nineveh. While prayer changes things, personal contact with individuals could allow God to change Jonah's heart. Jonah didn't want the people to have a chance to repent -- *and he also didn't want to face his own need to repent.* God often tells us that we must go to places that we might not have a strong desire. Often we change the directions God gives us to go. While there are obviously numbers of ways to make disciples, Jesus tells us to "go and make disciples." Notice the word "go." "Go" means "to move, to proceed, to depart, to be about to do, to circulate, to tend, to be guided, to reach, to avail;" in other words, to *go.*

Without a doubt, God has directed his people to go and get things done for him, but our many definitions (and interpretations) of God's command to "go" have enabled many of us to run from the call on our lives. With all the innovations in ministry and the new forms of service, we've taken some of the responsibility and personal contact out of our Christian walk.

For a long time in the church, things were pretty simple. The gospel singing group the Winans sang a song years back called "Bring Back The Days of Yea and Nay." The song is a reflection of life in our churches today. We have so many gray areas in which to hide that it's almost impossible to distinguish what is real from what is not. We've allowed the many forms of lukewarmness to become the norms of our churches and lives. Because of our faults, the results have visited our children. The generation of young people that have followed appear to be the most troubled and confused in the history of the American church.

It's easy to hide our dysfunction from the world, but we can't hide it from ourselves. Our youth have a double-edged sword to walk on. The world they live in is already filled with contradictions. One day they see people marching for safer streets. "Stop the Violence" rallies at our city halls are hyped. The next week the same people are organizing a pro-abortion rally to maintain the right to kill their own children. Then they come to church and hear us sing about the love of God, and how that love flows through us all. In the time it takes us to leave the building we show our hate for one another in ways that we "color" in political and ethnic terms.

I recall speaking to a group of young people at a retreat in the mountains of Colorado. I was asked to conduct a particular class that was made up of teens, ages 14 to 18. When I arrived at the camp site I realized that I was the only black person there. That didn't bother me, because it happens quite often. I did, however, have several parents ignore me as I tried to make conversation. That happens quite often, too.

The group was a bit restless, as teens tend to be at Christian retreats. I felt led to dump my written presentation and discuss their everyday lives. One of the questions I asked them led to a very telling discussion. I asked how many of them had heard their parents talk about black people in a derogatory manner at home. About 80% of them raised their hands. I then asked had they heard there parents use the "n-word" to describe black people at home. About the same number raised their hands. We then discussed how those attitudes at home directly conflicted with what they heard from parents and other adults at church.

I will never forget the honesty and emotion in that room. Many of the parents who were present at the camp commented to me after dinner that evening that their children returned from my session with them genuinely excited about what they had learned. Still, I was sad they had to go to a camp to learn the truth about loving one another.

A Problem of Color, or a Problem of the Heart?

So many of our shortcomings would be eliminated if we'd only heed the command of God to go be with "those people." Being in personal contact with others does

something that praying for folks at a distance can never do.
I'm a great supporter of financial backing for the work and
people of God, but it is imperative in this day that we
understand the importance of being in one another's
presence. Physical, personal contact allows something to
happen that God desires: *we get to know one another!*
   If we never get to know one another the foolishness that
we have held on to in our churches in America will never
stop. So much of it is created by the fear of the unknown. We
just don't know each other. We say we don't have anything
in common, but we know better.
   First of all, we have our race in common. Let's be clear
on something. We are all part of the same race: the human
race. We call this thing that divides us "race," but the reality
is we are all the same species. We have different colors, but
we are all the same race. The issue here is not really our
color, either. I've heard whites comment on the great tans
they have. If the color of black folks' skin is so deplorable,
why do white people lay in the sun for hours to get a tan?
(Tan is just light brown anyway.)
   Is the issue really color? The same type of hatred that we
exhibit toward each other in America is duplicated and worse
in Europe among people of the same color. Bosnia is an
unfortunate example. Same color, different politics. In Africa
black people have killed those of the same color by the
thousands in places like Rwanda and Burundi.
   In our country our hate just plays itself out more
prominently in the color game. But this has never been a
problem of color. It's always been a problem of the heart.
   I'll say it again: *what we are experiencing is a heart
problem.* If we look deeper than color we'd realize that this
dilemma is not about skin, it's about sin. Sin in our hearts
allows us to go through life feeling that we are better than
someone else because our skin is lighter or darker. Sin makes
us feel we have the right to hate others because the past may

affirm it. Sin tells our hearts we are justified in our beliefs of
superiority and hate.

God told Jonah to go to the city because the people
needed to hear a word from heaven. But they needed to hear
it from a man who had no reason to want to help them,
largely for that man's sake. I'm sure God knew this wasn't
Jonah's first choice for a vacation, but he also wanted to give
Jonah an opportunity to get his heart right. It was an
opportunity for Jonah not only to be a hero for God, but also
to be free from the hate that made him less than what God
desired for him.

Today, God desires us to go to each other. There are a
number of reasons we need to be in each other's presence.
The world is searching for heroes. There seems to be a deep
desire in us to experience the power of heroism. Otherwise,
why would we flock to movies to see one individual take on
an army and win? The glory and majesty that comes from a
victory against the odds turns us on; it warms a fire within us
that everyday life cannot. Today, we're desperately in need
of heroes.

There are armies of hatred, fear, mistrust,
misunderstanding and doubt marching down our church
aisles every Sunday. Yet we stand in our pulpits and sit in
our pews allowing our foes to rape and pillage our land.
Where are the warriors? Who has the courage to make the
changes that will conquer the sin that has risen to God's
notice?

God is giving us a chance to be the heroes of our
generation. However, we can't be the heroes God is calling
us to be unless we go to where the battle is.

The Right Word at the Right Time

The people need to hear a word from God. God told
Jonah, "Proclaim to [Nineveh] the message I give you." It is
not enough to go into a setting that God sends us. We must

go with a word from the Lord that is specific to the time and generation he is sending us to.

So often we find people in the right place but proclaiming the wrong word. Missionaries have done an invaluable service in times past across the world, but it is also true many have done untold damage. Many missionaries took more than the word of God with them to foreign soil; they took the customs of their culture. In many instances, those customs made the Gospel sound as though color or culture gave the missionaries a marked superiority over those they were there to serve. While God's instructions were "Tell them the word I give you," many missionaries added "other" words that changed the results of the mission. That mentality is still being demonstrated in the Body of Christ and it must be stopped.

The message God gives us for today must be one that is direct from God's heart to the heart of the people we visit. *Our* words will not do; we must give the word of God. Our words can confuse or alienate those God wants to reach. Our words will serve our own purposes, not God's purpose. God's word will heal situations; our words will only make new wounds.

God's word is anointed to break the chains that have bound us for centuries. In addition to freeing those to whom God sends us, our very obedience in going to those who are different gives us an opportunity for freedom ourselves.

There is nothing more crippling than to be a child of the King and still be bound to hate. Jonah knew what that was like. He knew God in his greatness. He had experienced the overwhelming power of his love and mercy. He had experience with the Lord that could not be denied. That experience allowed him, even in the middle of a great tempest, to brag to sinners concerning the greatness of God. Nevertheless, he was bound by the hatred he held in his heart for the people of Nineveh.

History Lessons

Looking at the history of the two cultures we might be tempted to say that the man had a right to hate them. My research seems to indicate that these folks had different skin color, but that was not Jonah's reason for hating the Ninevites. While skin color might have made it easier to recognize the city dwellers, the reason for Jonah's hate was much deeper.

As we discussed earlier in the book, these folks in Nineveh had a history of running over the children of Israel. The pain that Nineveh had placed upon the children of Israel still ached in Jonah's heart and mind. Time had not healed the wound that the people of Nineveh had inflicted. They had, on more than one occasion, devastated Jonah's ancestors. While these incidents were history by Jonah's time, Jonah felt them as if they were happening to him.

All that being said, God still hadn't given Jonah permission to hate the people of Nineveh. As a matter of fact, God had told Jonah that "its [Nineveh's] wickedness has come up before me." (Jonah 1:2) He let Jonah know that Nineveh's time of sinning was up, and he was now ready to deal with them for the sins they had committed. How ironic that God would use a man who was considered weak and inferior by the Ninevites to proclaim such a powerful judgment against them.

Blacks and other ethnic groups in America have harbored great animosity, and even hate, against whites for wrongs of the past. No doubt we should look upon the history of our great land and study the extent of these wrongs to understand why so many feel this way. While scripture does not condone our holding any resentment in our hearts, let's try to understand for a moment why some of it is hard to release.

So often I've heard white people say, "Why do they (black people) keep bringing up those things from the past? I wasn't around in the time of slavery. I didn't lynch anybody in the 50's. Let's just forget it and go on from here." To many people that argument sounds relatively reasonable. However, when we take into consideration the manner in which our society remembers, celebrates, teaches, rewards and places value upon the European history and culture while virtually ignoring the history and importance of African Americans, it's small wonder ill feelings persist. In addition, America won't let blacks forget the past. So often the actions of the present tell us that the past is not forgotten.

Like Jonah reasoned in his heart, many blacks have reasoned that "those people" (the phrase works both ways) have been on top for generations. They not only took the land from those who were here first, they came and took us from our land and enslaved us for centuries. Many of us feel that it isn't fair to say that those things we learned in school were not important. But they indeed are important to the history of our country. However, so much of history is left untold. Much of what has not been taught in our schools in the United States is the cause of the attitudes of superiority by whites. Many others have attitudes that smell of indifference. Why shouldn't they, since they believe blacks or other people of color haven't contributed anything to this country anyway? It is sad to know that most whites in this country couldn't tell me (or you) five African Americans who have contributed great things to our land. They think all we do is jump high, run fast and eat watermelon.

But probably the greatest travesty is how white theologians and Bible teachers have attempted to eliminate blacks from the history of the Scriptures. So many of those who confess to love God and all his people have changed the truth of Scripture into a lie.

William D. McKissic, Sr. and Anthony T. Evans cite numerous occasions where white scholars have changed the truth of scripture to eliminate or lessen the role of blacks in their book *Beyond Roots II* (Renaissance Publications). These documented cases are at the root of much of the distrust many blacks hold for whites and the church in general. McKissic and Evans argue that, if anything, the witness of Genesis 10 offers evidence that blacks played a highly significant role throughout the Bible. Further, their civilizations shaped much of the ancient Near East if the Bible is to be believed.

The irony brought out so brilliantly by McKissic and Evans is that many whites in the American evangelical church actually believe that blacks have no history worth mentioning. McKissic and Evans call for the healing process to begin with the teaching of the truth, starting with the Scriptures. (Go buy the book.)

It's sad that whole people groups and their accomplishments are never mentioned in the history books in our schools. Usually when a person sees no reason to admire another it is very difficult to form any kind of relationship. That's why whites are so eager to accept a black athlete or entertainer into their neighborhood or family. Their accomplishment generates the admiration that gives birth to the desire to establish and nurture a relationship. That admiration crosses color lines.

Think about that: admiration breaks down barriers. Usually that's how we develop relationships with those who will become our mates. We don't really know them but there is something about them that makes us want to know them better. Some degree of admiration is crucial in any relationship. If whites see blacks and other people of color as non-contributors to the society in which we live, no relationship of substance will be pursued. The result is ongoing prejudice and indifference in our land.

Let me suggest that if you need a reason to feel good about those of different cultures than yours, go to your nearest library or bookstore and acquire some books on black inventors. You will be amazed at the number of everyday items you use that blacks invented.

We fault the world for its omissions in history books, but to change the color of people in God's Holy Word so as not to show God's participation in the lives of Africans in Bible robs everyone of the truth. That thievery has weakened the Body and ushered countless numbers away from the cross.

How to Heal Hatred

With so much history that demonstrates mistreatment it's no wonder we think we can justify hating each other. The problem with such an attempt is that God never gave us permission to hate one another. To you people of color who look at whites with hate and anger, I must say this: you are wrong. The sins of the past don't give us a right to hate.

However, I do believe that many of my brothers and sisters must listen today to the Word of the Lord as it is proclaimed through this black and other people of color. The word God declares today is this: "Your sin has come up before me. The sin of racism will not be tolerated in the House of God. It stinks in God's nostrils and severely weakens the Body of Christ. Repent of the sin of racial prejudice and be healed."

I must admit to you that much of what God has called me to do the last few years is not what I've preferred to do. I've had some white associates over the years, as well as a couple of good friends who are white. And while I've never made an attempt to avoid anyone, our society has made it clear that I'm more welcome with my own kind.

My family taught me to love everybody, but never to trust white people. Coming from my cultural and personal history, that should be understood. But, God in his infinite wisdom and plan has put me in the lives of many whites. That has proven to be a form of healing for me, if not for everyone with whom I've had some type of relationship.

I know now that I can indeed trust some whites just like I can trust some Blacks, Native Americans, Asians, and Hispanics. Not once have I changed my appearance, tastes, opinions or preferences. However, I have had the opportunity to be delivered from a deep-seated hatred that goes back farther than I can remember. It was not only a hate for those who enslaved my ancestors, but also their ancestors who cheated my grandparents out of the things that should have rightfully been theirs. It was a hate that came from all the years of watching television and reading articles that never included heroes that looked like me; a hate that caused me as a child to wish I was something that I was not in order to be special.

This same hate was fueled when I attended college and my white Christian brothers and sisters would rarely speak or fellowship with me and other black Christians on campus. During my adult life, that hate grew into a giant after countless personal events proved that years of laws, marches, meetings, speeches, and hope had done little to change things. Being a Christian didn't change it. Being college-educated didn't change it. Having a good job didn't change it. Making money and investing it wisely never changed an thing. If I dressed the way whites thought was acceptable, that didn't change a thing. Hating whites more didn't change matters either.

Only when I accepted the call of God to go the people I hated did he heal me. They were not all healed, and neither will they be in our churches, as we will discuss in the next and final chapter. But, this was also my opportunity. If America's Body of Christ ever wants to be healed, one truth stands as a testament of God's plan: *we still have to go to the city.*

We all have our Nineveh. Nineveh is not always a people. It can be a person, place or thing that we loathe. It isn't always a group that lives across town. It's not always the culture that dresses funny or eats those strange foods. Nineveh can be right in our own homes. It can be part of our own history and not show on the outside. It may not stand sit or talk right in front of us, but it's always there lurking in our conscience. We believe we can run from it but it's always there, waiting to be dealt with.

Jonah spent precious time running from the very thing that he needed to face. He needed to face the great city not just for Nineveh's sake, but for his own as well.

Many of us are doing the same. Like Jonah, we must understand that the only way we will be able to accomplish the will of God for our lives is to go to Nineveh. We can never accomplish our purpose until we deal with the Ninevites. Running away from it will not solve the stinging memories that haunt us.

God's way of escape has more to do with confrontation than running. The more time we waste running the less time we have to accomplish our task: we still have to stand, sit, walk, talk and pray together and find out what makes each other tick.

If we don't, we will never have the opportunity to be whole.

Chapter Ten
The Spirit of Jonah

But Jonah was greatly displeased and became angry...But the Lord replied, "Have you any right to be angry?" (Jonah 4:1,4)

It appears a hero is born in Jonah chapter 3:
Jonah obeyed the word of the Lord and went to Nineveh. (Jonah 3:3)
We find the reluctant prophet in the midst of the very people he was bound and determined to avoid, even if it meant his life and call. Scripture also indicates not only was he in the presence of these people, but this time he also followed the directions given him by the Father concerning his message.
He proclaimed: "Forty more days and Nineveh will be overturned." (Jonah 3:4)
After all that Jonah had experienced, there he was among the people he despised. He was surrounded by Ninevites on their turf. Still, he was proclaiming God's word to them.

Jonah had wasted valuable time avoiding his destiny, but now he was in the place he should have been all along. No doubt that in the time it took him to reach the city things had gotten worse in Nineveh. More evil had been accomplished in the sight of God. The city government had become more corrupt. Sexual sin and all forms of moral decay had probably become an increasingly bigger problem. All of this occurred while Jonah spent precious time running from Nineveh.

Jonah may have never understood this, but his purpose would never be accomplished until he obeyed the word of the Lord. In Jonah's case, obedience meant complying to

God's wish for him regarding his mission to Nineveh. Little did he seem to know that the obedience he avoided was the very key to his own deliverance, for Jonah was yoked with a weight much heavier than even could imagine. His hate for the people of the city was a great hindrance to his own fulfillment. With all his success, he still was not whole because of the yoke of hate fixed to his soul.

Even though nurturing hate was the path he had chosen, Jonah got right to the task at hand preaching to the very people he would see perish. Amazingly, the words from this seemingly inferior individual touched the hearts of the citizens of Nineveh in a remarkable way. Because of Jonah's obedience to the will of God,

The Ninevites believed God. (Jonah 3:5)

It doesn't seem to make much sense, does it? A guy walks into a sinful city equipped with nothing more than words and he gets amazing results. This man who had no clout, with obviously no connections, and part of a culture considered to be inferior by "the locals," had an impact.

We must realize Nineveh was no ordinary place:

Nineveh was a very important city... (Jonah 3:3)

This community was not looking for direction or purpose. They were already important, with a rich commerce and culture. Business was booming and they were a military power with a history of glorious victories. They even knew religion as part of their culture. The walls around their nation were strong and they felt secure in their existence.

Jonah, in obedience to God, walked into the city and spoke words that would normally draw laughter. The response was astounding: *The Ninevites believed God!* Not only did they believe, *they responded in faith* to Israel's God.

So On Your Next Visit to Nineveh....

God is calling us to fulfill our purpose in the land we occupy. We may be called to enter into a relationship with individuals that are totally foreign to us. God may ask us to enter relationships with folks who don't look, speak or think like us.

In our ministries sometimes, we are called to say words that make little sense when you compare them to the complicated, sophisticated, strategically planned society in which we live. We may be accused of everything from being a "holy roller" to simply being out of step with reality. But if what we share is the word of God for this time, an amazing thing will happen: *the people will believe God.*

I'm convinced that much of what we call the work of the Lord is *only* work. It may be good work. It might even be contemporary, state of the art, divinity-certified, denominationally-approved, oil-bathed and modestly dressed. But if it's not backed up by the direction and power of the almighty God, it's just work. We confuse God's work with ours, often calling our work "the work of the Lord" when in reality it's work of the flesh, a poor and powerless substitute.

God's word has the power to even reach those in political office, you know:

> *When the news reached the king of Nineveh, he rose from his throne...(Jonah 3:6)*

Notice that the word of God didn't affect the seat of government first. Ordinary citizens from all walks of life were the first to be moved by Jonah's message. The word of the Lord caused a street level call to repentance before the political powers were even aware of what was going on:

> *The Ninevites believed God. They declared a fast, and all of them, from the greatest to the least, put on sackcloth. (Jonah 3:5)*

Yes, God is interested in the seats of authority in the land. But God won't ask permission from the legislative branch to start revival in the land.

There are also revivals in the Body of Christ that don't start with bishops, pastors or deacon boards. There *are* times when the pew receives the message before the pulpit.

God in his sovereign way often starts his move with ordinary people. The divine move that will combat the sin of racial hatred in our land will probably not start with the leadership of the organized church. Leaders have come and gone without the slightest mention of this shameful sin. Many of our leaders are so intimidated by the past, present and future that we refuse to yield totally to God's command to "love one another." We often fear what might happen to our ecclesiastical careers should we take a "controversial" stance, even if it agrees with the Holy Scripture. Sunday after Sunday and sermon after sermon the road leads to this discussion, but a detour is taken that avoids the obvious.

Likewise, the problem won't be overcome by our political process. We spend so much time trying to convince ourselves that God is affiliated more with one political party than the other. In reality, there are Christians and sinners voting, campaigning and making promises they can't keep in both main parties and all the new ones we'll probably start before the end of the century. We label ourselves "liberal" or "conservative." Neither term is biblical, nor should they be looked upon as such. Jesus obviously taught truths that can be termed "conservative" by our limited vocabulary. However, much of what he taught us to do in terms of the poor is branded today as "liberal" thinking.

Let's thank God for our wonderful system that allows us the right to vote for the candidates and amendments of our choice. In recent months it has been proven that much of what we've been taking for granted is in jeopardy. The overturning of Colorado's Amendment 2, which denied special rights to homosexuals, has many citizens frightened. Are we heading into a time where are votes only count if they reflect the wishes of those in the Supreme Court? Let's hope and pray that we're not.

Countdown to Revival

As a minister of the Gospel of Jesus Christ I can say without any hesitation the greatest feeling in the world is to witness the response of an individual or individuals to the invitation to salvation. Preaching or teaching the word of God is an honor in itself. The added responsibility of calling souls to repentance is both humbling and exhilarating.

Jonah was in the midst of a full blown tidal wave of repentance and revival. From the streets to the palace, commoners, royalty and animals alike were dressed in sackcloth crying out to God. (The practice of dressing animals in sackcloth and using them in some ceremonies of mourning was customary in the ancient Near East.)

I can only imagine the look on Jonah's face as he watched the reaction of his audience. The proof of the call and anointing of God was all around him. So great was the repentance in Nineveh that scripture says,

When God saw what they did and how they turned from their evil ways, he had compassion and did not bring upon them the destruction he had threatened. (Jonah 3:10)

The nation of Nineveh did not just fast because they were humiliated. They fasted because they were truly sorry for their sin. It was the moral life (or lack of one) of the Ninevites that moved God to compassion.

In *The Interpreter's Bible*, William Scarlett wrote,

It was as though the people said, "If we repent who can tell if God will not relent?" The people were not appealing to a law but to a Person. A law is inexorable; a person may change his mind...As Joel (2:13 -14) had said: "Rend your heart, and not your garments, and turn

unto the Lord your God....Who knoweth if he will return
and repent, and leave behind a blessing behind him?"
(*The Interpreter's Bible*, v. 6, p. 890-1; Abingdon Press,
1956)

This is a spiritual fact: God changes the final outcome for
each of us as we allow him to change our hearts, and then
our behavior. When we repent -- literally, change our
direction -- God changes his divine judgment concerning us.
Righteousness and mercy are both part of God's nature,
which is unchanging. Thankfully, our response in Jesus
Christ to God's unchanging nature can determine a change in
his judgment of us.

The Fear of Success
The repentance of Nineveh should signal the climax to a
successful evangelistic campaign for Jonah. Victory is
written all over this story.
Unfortunately, that's not how the saga ends. For as soon
as God begins to move in the land that was foreign to the
prophet, an astounding part of Jonah's spirit was revealed.
*But Jonah was greatly displeased and became angry.
(Jonah 4:1)*
In the midst of what probably was the greatest move of
God ever seen in Nineveh, the man of God responsible
became irate. His mood is described as "greatly displeased"
and "angry." Could it be he was upset that he didn't receive
an honorarium for his services? Could it be he wasn't given
an award by the revival committee? If everybody and
everything was fasting and praying, what type of results was
he looking for anyway?
*He prayed to the Lord, "O Lord, is this not what I
said when I was still at home? That is why I was so quick
to flee to Tarshish. I knew that you are a gracious and
compassionate God, slow to anger and abounding in*

love, a God who relents from sending calamity." (Jonah 4:2)

Can you believe what you just read? Jonah was not upset because some souls were not moving to God fast enough. He was mad because *the people believed God.* The entire fourth chapter of the book that bears his name is an account of his displeasure. It was an anger that could not tolerate God's grace being shown to "those people" he considered to be heathen.

The inevitable and tragic conclusion is that *Jonah had learned nothing* from his earlier calamities. He was the same man on the inside, even though he had obeyed God outwardly.

He didn't point his rage at the Ninevites; instead, he speaks directly to God. As a prophet of God he knows how to approach God. He prays, "Lord, this is what I told you from the start. I knew you'd be merciful. That's why I ran."

While we may be amazed at the results of the disobedient prophet's sermon, Jonah was not. He exclaims to God, "I know you, God. I know your way with grace and mercy." The prophet was well acquainted with the Master of all living things, and Jonah didn't want to give God an opportunity to be God in a way that didn't suit his desires. The reason Jonah ran in the first place was that he could predict what God was going to do with grace and mercy if given the opportunity. The last thing Jonah wanted was for God to use him to give "those people" in Nineveh an opportunity at life.

Jonah makes another interesting comment about the character of God by describing God as "a God who relents from sending calamity." (Jonah 4:2b) To "relent" means "to soften in temper or become less severe." Unlike the image many of us have of God with huge lightning bolts in his hand ready and waiting to blow us out of our skins, Jonah knew the deep compassion of the Creator. Although God is able to judge in a severe way, he would rather see us repent and avoid the wrath that is to come. The prophet Jeremiah affirmed this character trait of God:

>   ...and if that nation I warned repents of its evil, then I will relent and not inflict on it the disaster I had planned. (Jeremiah 18:8)

The Spirit of Jonah

The spirit of Jonah is indeed a peculiar one. Nevertheless it's quite familiar to us Americans. Jonah was a practitioner of "selective evangelism." This type of ministry chooses who should be blessed, saved, delivered or given any opportunity to adhere to God's grace.

The spirit of Jonah can be hard to spot. Those guilty of exhibiting the spirit of Jonah can be servants of God. They may have a calling on their lives and should not always be confused with non-believers or false prophets, for those who harbor it could have a relationship with God and enjoy success in ministry.

For those in the church, the spirit of Jonah is not reserved for those who are new in the Body of Christ. On the contrary, individuals with the spirit of Jonah are usually set in their ways and careful to avoid an overt display separatism. Except for the problems that move these individuals to action, they normally exhibit an ordinary lifestyle -- unlike a supremacist or the like who openly and purposely shouts his or her racist rhetoric.

Those who are burdened with the spirit of Jonah are often moved to believe that things should be the way they see it, without exception. The spirit of Jonah can rest upon individuals or groups who have traditionally been oppressed or those who come from the oppressor category.

Jonah himself was a member of the oppressed. Years of being a member of the downtrodden had caused him to be extremely bitter, narrow-minded and unforgiving.

Entrenched in his heart was also a pain that the oppressor
could not understand. Yes, he was a servant of God, but he
also was human. His humanity had scars that the oppressor's
sword could never inflict. History had left scars that were
deeply imbedded in his conscience. Those that had made
their fortune, fame and comfort on the very backs of his
ancestors were enjoying some riches that could have
belonged to him.

Many of our fellow Americans find themselves in that
number. The hurt is so deep it blinds them to their own hate,
a hate that sometimes motivates to great heights, but always
anchors the soul to murky depths. Watching in contempt as
the dominant culture enjoys a prosperity their people have
seldom known, the pain grows worse.

Even after salvation there is something in many of us that
won't allow trust for those who were part of the destruction
of our forefathers. Not allowing the power of the cross the
opportunity to heal us, we remain trapped by the high walls
of hatred.

The oppressor's hate comes from a different perspective.
His hate comes from a three-part combination of fear, dislike
and superiority. The fear comes from the feeling that those
who were oppressed may somehow gain the power and
knowledge that has historically belonged with the oppressor.
With that kind of power the oppressed will at least share in
the wealth and power. The oppressors' worst fears tell them,
"If 'those people' become empowered, they may do to us
what we did to them." Some oppressors take their fear to the
ultimate level, violently opposing any advancement of the
oppressed. That fear forces them to deny the oppressed in
whatever way they feel necessary, including the burning and
destruction of churches, homes and dreams.

The dislike of the oppressed leaves a very bitter taste.
The oppressor rarely wants to become a part of the
oppressed's history, present or future, so he designs things of

importance in the community to affirm his own tastes, likes and values. The culture, creations and values of the oppressed are either considered worthless, novelties, or worse, are stolen away and credited to the oppressor's community. The oppressed never become a recognized part of the community until the oppressor dictates the "acceptable" standards for their inclusion.

The oppressor's feeling of superiority over the oppressed is the most remarkable part of the triune, for it is this piece that drives the entire machine. You'll recall that "superiority" means "to be greater than." The oppressor usually finds a way to remind the oppressed that they are, and always will be, "lesser than." The word "minority" itself means "lesser than, outnumbered, less than half, the losing side or the lesser part." Too often, the connotation follows that the minority is not only less than in number but also in importance. The oppressor will almost always find an excuse for the success of the oppressed, taking credit when the oppressed succeed and gloating when they fail. The oppressor seldom wants to reside in the same community as the oppressed. Economic accomplishments of the oppressed rarely matter to the oppressor.

The oppressor will usually maintain this sense of superiority by teaching his offspring they are superior. Those lessons can be taught intentionally or by example. Should the oppressed begin to attain the same heights as the oppressor, the oppressor will usually change the standards by which they measure superiority.

All these dynamics were playing into Jonah's feelings toward Nineveh as he worked through being one of those whose people had been oppressed by the harsh hand of that great city. But Jonah's hatred was so frustrated by God's mercy shown to "those people" that life itself lost meaning for the prophet:

*"Now O Lord, take away my life, for it is better for
me to die than to live." (Jonah 4:3)*

The "A-List" of Grace

Jonah was so angry about God's mercy toward Nineveh
that he stated before his Creator he would rather die than live
in a world that would allow "those people" a chance at God's
grace.

Ironically, it was the same grace Jonah himself craved.
God's grace can appear in many different forms. Most of us
place wealth, health, peace, contentment, houses and land on
the "A-list" of evidence of God's grace. So why is it, then,
that we have members of the Body of Christ who feel that
the grace "A-list" should be reserved only for a select group?
That was the question God put to Jonah.

*But the Lord replied, "Have you any right to be
angry?" (Jonah 4:4)*

God questioned Jonah as a parent would a sulking child,
with a fatherly attitude that assisted the prophet as he
searched his feelings.

God displayed the same concern when he questioned
Cain about his anger against Abel in Genesis 4. Cain was
angry because God rejected his sacrifice. However, in
Genesis 4:7, God revealed the reason Cain's sacrifice was
not accepted:

*"If you do what is right, will you not be accepted?
But if you do not do what is right, sin is crouching at
your door; it desires to have you, but you must master
it." (Genesis 4:7)*

Cain blamed Abel for his failure and anger, but God
made it clear that Cain's problem was within himself. Cain,
like Jonah, had a heart problem. And like Cain, Jonah failed
to heed the advice of a loving God.

Jonah, like a spoiled child stomping off to a corner to
pout, shows his lack of maturity.

*Jonah went out and sat down at a place east of he
city. There he made himself a shelter, sat in its shade and
waited to see what would happen to the city. (Jonah 4:5)*
Jonah had passed through the whole city to reach its
eastern side, a three-day journey. It had been two days since
Jonah had first witnessed the repentance of the people. Jonah
didn't want to be in the city to be an eyewitness to the revival
he had sparked. His opportunity to be released from the hate
within him was inside the city, but Jonah chose to camp
outside the city and wait to see if God would change his
mind and punish the Assyrians within the walls of Nineveh.

We live in a time when God is tearing down walls that
have divided us since the inception of our nation. He has
called together men and women to assist in this great move.
There is no doubt that what we have seen in the faces of
many brothers and sisters is true love and repentance. Many
have put their lives and money where their mouths are, and
we are spending the time necessary to learn about and
learning to love our Christian family of all cultures.

Unfortunately, the spirit of Jonah has driven some
members of our family outside the walls of the city. While
many of us bask in the glow of God's deliverance, many
others choose to watch from a considerable distance. Some
who invest in this movement by marching, singing, giving
resources and even preaching have shied away from being an
active part of the revival. Like Jonah, they sit outside of the
flow of the Spirit and wait to see if God will change his
mind. Privately, they hope that some kind of mistake has
happened.

As the book of Jonah comes to an end we find Jonah
outside the city desiring death once again. This time,
however, Jonah's sorrow was over the withering of a plant
that God had provided to shelter him from the scorching sun.
God used the plant to explain his love for the people of
Nineveh to Jonah, even though the prophet seemed to be a

lost cause. The plant in question was probably a castor oil plant. Its leaves would have supplied enough shade to give Jonah protection from the harmful rays of the sun. The plant had grown suddenly at God's command, just as the ocean had raged, and the fish had swallowed and later spit Jonah. When the plant first appeared, it had changed Jonah's attitude from anger to delight. But the next morning, Jonah discovered the vine had died. The heat of the sirocco (the desert wind, not the Volkswagen) burned his brow. God had created a worm to destroy the very thing that Jonah was enjoying in the midst of his disobedience. Jonah became angry – again -- because of the destruction of this plant.

God asked the question that we should ponder today:

But God said to Jonah, "Do you have a right to be angry about the vine?" (Jonah 4:9a)

The plant that Jonah was counting on for comfort stands for those things that comfort us today. We are always up in arms about our possessions. From our homes to our pets, we Americans are constantly whining about our rights to protect what is "ours." Jonah replied to God's question just as we do when our possessions or comforts are threatened.

"I do," he said. "I am angry enough to die." (Jonah 4:9b)

Jonah wanted God to know he felt the plant deserved mercy – and that was exactly the lesson God was preparing for his prophet:

But the Lord said, "You have been concerned about this vine, though you did not tend it or make it grow. It sprang up overnight and died overnight. But Nineveh has more than a hundred and twenty thousand people who cannot tell their right hand from their left, and many cattle as well. Should I not be concerned about that great city?" (Jonah 4:10 , 11)

Like Jonah, we cry for mercy when we lose something that is precious to us. In most cases, like Jonah, we have done nothing to nurture this thing so dear to our heart. Yet we fight with all we have for its existence. The reality is, we have what we have because of the mercy and grace of the Almighty. Jonah, too, was capable of great compassion for something that lasted only a few hours and had no future life. He could cry for mercy on behalf of vegetation, yet was unwilling that God should be merciful to people.

How can we, as Christians who are the very object of God's mercy, not understand the love and mercy God has for all people? Yet everyday we show God what is truly important to us in this country. We show more love to things than to our fellow man.

Some of us, like Jonah, are at a point of no return. We could be at the place where we feel that no matter what God does, our minds are made up concerning those of different cultures. We may see more value in things that we have never labored for than the precious souls for whom Christ died. If so, we must also understand that the spirit of Jonah is alive and well within us. We should strive not to be one of the vessels which takes this virus through the bloodstream of the Body of Christ.

God spoke to Jonah concerning the 120,000-plus individuals "who could not tell their right hand from their left." There is some debate among Bible scholars concerning who God had in mind in reference to that phrase, and I won't bore you with the arguments here. Still, I choose to believe God was talking about small children as this group; youngsters who had not been affected by the stain of hate or the prejudice of historical facts. These little ones most deserved a chance to choose which way they should go. While adults had spent time mocking God with their lifestyles, the children were innocent. God tried to show Jonah as well we today that these souls are much more significant than most of the issues and material things we fight and die over. But the spirit of Jonah doesn't care about the children of those they despise. It only cares for itself.

How can we who are pardoned by the sacrifice of the Son of God ever forget the grace and mercy shown us? Yet some of us do.

Will you forget?

This country is waiting for the church to be the shining example of God's word, but we rarely display the attitudes and actions that would prove us to be his own.

What is our role in this ongoing journey? Will we ignore God's voice today?

Will we run in obedience to God, or away from his call on our lives?

Only time will tell. Only we can write the final chapter.